"If you need to be rei   s
guided study of Eph.   J
struggle to love the people in your life well, this study will remind you of
the selfless love available through His Spirit. I've watched Lara live out the
message of being rooted in God's love so she can graciously love others
through unimaginable trials. You are in good hands."

 —HEATHER MACFADYEN, host of the God Centered Mom podcast

"Lara is a woman of God who deeply roots herself in His Word. She desires
God's truth to penetrate the very fibers of her days, affecting how she ministers in her home and in the world. She has a way with words that can grip
your heart and lead you into the throne room of our King. I'm certain this
walk through Ephesians will bless all who take the journey."

 —CHRYSTAL EVANS HURST, author of *She's Still There*

"Lara is one of the most talented writers I know. She is a wordsmith, and
her ability to connect people to God through words is a gift to all who
encounter them. But Lara is more than just a word girl. She is a faithful
disciple of Christ, a gospel-centric teacher of the Word, and a woman bent
on following and honoring God with all she has and does."

 —KATIE ORR, creator of the FOCUSed15 Bible study series

"Lara Williams is a deep well. She's one of those rare people whose wisdom,
words, and life are so rooted in Christ that every interaction with her leaves
me wanting more of Him."

 —KAT LEE, founder and author of *Hello Mornings*,
and founder of InspiredtoAction.com

"Lara Williams is passionate in her pursuit of Jesus, and it comes through every spoken word and line written. She is rooted first in the love of her Savior, and it overflows to everyone around her. Lara's gift lies within her ability to walk with her audience, hold her story open-handed, and point them to Jesus. I can't think of a more appropriate study for her to pen than this one."

—STACEY THACKER, author of *Is Jesus Worth It?*

"I'm so grateful Lara shared her exploration of Ephesians with us! This study was a much-needed refresher for me on the gentle and gracious ways God pulls us close. Lara writes with such humility and tenderness that you feel as though you're sitting around the coffee table—sisters encouraging each other. We need more like this."

—CHRISTA WELLS, singer/songwriter

"Lara Williams has a gift for unpacking the Word in a way that makes it easy to digest. *Rooted* does just that. The way Lara guides the reader through Ephesians brings Scripture to life in a fresh way."

—LIZ GRIFFIN, speaker, writer, and pastor

"Lara has the uncanny ability to make me laugh, cry, and hunger deeply for God all in one sitting. I'm so excited for *Rooted* to get in the hands of women everywhere so they too can encounter the love of Christ in a way that changes them from the inside out. *Rooted* draws us into the heart of God, giving us space to meet face to face with Him in His unchanging Word, allowing truth to inform us and transform us."

—FRANCIE WINSLOW, wife, mom, speaker, and writer

Rooted

going deep into God's
transforming love

Lara Williams

NEW HOPE®
PUBLISHERS

BIRMINGHAM, ALABAMA

New Hope® Publishers
PO Box 12065
Birmingham, AL 35202-2065
NewHopePublishers.com
New Hope Publishers is a division of Iron Stream Media.

Library of Congress Cataloging-in-Publication Data

Names: Williams, Lara, 1975- author.
Title: Rooted : going deep into God's transforming love / Lara Williams.
Description: First [edition]. | Birmingham : New Hope Publishers, 2017.
Identifiers: LCCN 2017038969 | ISBN 9781625915375 (permabind)
Subjects: LCSH: Bible. Ephesians--Textbooks.
Classification: LCC BS2695.55 .W55 2017 | DDC 227/.5--dc23
LC record available at https://lccn.loc.gov/2017038969

ISBN-13: 978-1-62591-537-5

N184110 • 0118 • 2M1

DEDICATION

To my sisters in the Lord who have prayed, encouraged, spoken life, and reflected the love of Jesus to me in the every day. You know who you are.

> *[May] you, being rooted and grounded in love . . . have strength to comprehend with all the saints what is the breadth and length and height and depth, and to know the love of Christ that surpasses knowledge, that you may be filled with all the fullness of God.*
>
> —EPHESIANS 3:17–18

CONTENTS

ACKNOWLEDGMENTS

I have to begin by thanking my mama, who sacrificially helped me carry the daily tasks of life while I would step away to write the words and message in this study. Thank you, Mom. I'm in my forties and I still need you.

Thank you to my husband Adam and my three children Hailey, Bryson, and Ryan, who bear with me day in and day out. We do life messy and loud at times, but I'm so thankful I get to learn how to reflect the love of our Savior beside you. I pray God would continue to take us deeper into His love so we'd reflect Him . . . even through our crazy.

Thank you to the pastors and elders of Mercy Hill Church, my local church family. I cannot tell you enough how blessed I feel to sit under your teaching and leadership each week. Thank you for faithfully preaching the Word.

Many thanks to those near and far who have spurred me on in my writing journey. Your words of courage have pushed me to keep writing. Your inspiration has often refilled the ink in my pen. God has used you more than you know.

And though I feel like this could come across trite, I want to thank my Lord. *For real.* He's been so gracious and patient with me over the years. He has radically redeemed me in spite of me and continues to take me deeper in His love. *Father, thank You. Your love and grace overwhelms me.*

INTRODUCTION

LOVE DOWN AND OUT

A number of years ago, I instituted a two-part law for our home. My children were on their way to getting master's degrees in bickering, and my sanity needed protecting. So I told them, *rather loudly*, "We only have two things to do in this house and in our world. Two things. We love up and out. We love God and we love one another." I then proceeded to deliver a short sermon on love. And I may have asked for an "amen" or two when I was done preaching to their wide-eyed faces.

"Love up and out." It became my mantra. It became the plumb line I longed for us to use when evaluating how we were doing with this thing called life, because if love isn't at the root of what we say and do, then what we say and do is nothingness.

Fast-forward a few years. I had been praying about this book—the one in your hands. I had been asking God for His inspiration to write the words He would have me write for the people He would have read these pages. *Because what's the point of writing a book just to write a book?* I had been poring over Ephesians in my alone time with Him. Then, while sitting in church one cold, Sunday morning in February, it hit me. It's not "love up and out." It's "love down and out."

Love *down* and out.

God first loves us with a scandalous, ridiculously undeserved love. I *know* I don't deserve His love. Yet He bends down and raises me up. He comes to the outcast and rebel and invites us to dine with Him. He gives the blind sight. He makes the lame walk. He raises dead people from the grave. His love comes down and pierces us, the color of life spreading over our ashen skin. It's only when we truly experience the love of God that we can then love the world—beginning with those in our homes and spreading to the ends of the earth.

Love *down* and *out*.

We only get one chance here on this planet. One life. And I don't want to waste it. I want to be rooted deep in His love so that His love would flow out of me. I long for the love of Christ to change me from the inside out so that I might pour His love onto those around me. Without love, it's all a facade. Nothing really changes without love. People won't change. Families won't change. Churches won't change. And nations won't change.

So as you open these pages I join Paul in praying:

> *That according to the riches of [the Father's] glory he may grant you to be strengthened with power through his Spirit in your inner being, so that Christ may dwell in your hearts through faith—that you, being rooted and grounded in love, may have strength to comprehend with all the saints what is the breadth and length and height and depth, and to know the love of Christ that surpasses knowledge, that you may be filled with all the fullness of God.*
>
> —EPHESIANS 3:16–19

As we walk through these pages together, I pray God would root us deep into His love. And then, I pray we would pour out His love onto the world around us.

WHAT TO EXPECT

I don't want to simply write words. I don't want to create a pretty book with big leaves on the cover that tells stories to make you laugh and cry. Words that inspire you to post a picture on Instagram of your favorite page beside a cup of coffee with the caption, "Wow. #Truth." Well, I do want to do all of that, but not *only* that.

I want to write words that flow from the heart of God that He then miraculously uses to transform hearts. Words that infuse us with His love so we then go and make disciples, which then spurs others to go and make disciples, ad infinitum. So that's what I'm asking Him to do. I'm asking Him to set our spirits free from the sin that entangles us. I'm asking Him to loosen our feet and crush the boxes in which we try to contain Him. I'm asking Him to awaken us to the depth and height and magnitude of His love. It's a big ask, I suppose. But we have a big God.

So what should you expect from your time in this vehicle called a book? Well, expect to meet with the Father God through His Word in the power of His Spirit to the glory of Christ Jesus.

We're going to walk through the Book of Ephesians together, hopefully being awed by God's love along the way. Each day will have the same basic format. You will read a small portion of Ephesians. You will answer the same few questions and be encouraged to write out the day's text in your journal. Then I'll share what God showed me from the text. Finally, at the end of each day's study, I'll have a few questions for you to think and pray through, because . . . application. Each day should take less than thirty minutes—a small investment for enormous truths.

My hope and suggestion is that you would walk through this book in community. Grab a couple of friends, go through the week's readings, and then come together to discuss. Be authentic and encourage each other in your journeys. Be real with one another. Confess your sins to one another. Pray for one another. Then go tell others about His love.

week one

Immeasurable Love

Ephesians 1

DAY ONE

Ephesians 1:1–2

Here's our situation. We can't hear or see or understand the Almighty God without His gracious revelation to our human hearts. Have you heard the term "dumb sheep"? Yeah. That's us. So before we dive into the Word together each day, I want to encourage you to take a couple of minutes to simply breathe out life's distractions and invite our good God to speak to your soul. It may be a couple quick sentences like, "Lord, my life is a mess right now, but I know You are my hope. So please, speak and then give me ears to hear You." However it looks in your personal verbiage—*I love the word* verbiage—let's just be honest with Him and with ourselves. Let's speak the anxious places and expect to meet with Him through our time in His Word.

Did you talk to Him for a minute? If so, thou mayest proceed.

We'll start each day of our study by reading the text, writing the text in your journal, and then answering a couple of questions. After that, I've written a short commentary on the text followed by some personal questions for you to prayerfully answer. Simple enough, right?

Today we're only going to look at the first two verses of Paul's letter to the church at Ephesus.

Read Ephesians 1:1–2. Write these verses in your journal.

What does today's text reveal about God?

    God the Father:

God the Son (Jesus Christ):

God the Holy Spirit:

What does today's text reveal about humankind?

_____ God prompts:

(This is the space for you to write down anything the Lord pressed upon you through your initial read of the text. It may be a word or phrase. It may be a conviction or truth. Whatever jumped off the page. If you don't have anything to write, that's OK too.)

Growing up, I wanted to be a writer. But . . . I couldn't write. I would sit at my desk with a crisp, new black-and-white composition notebook spread open before me, dreams welling up in my young spirit about being an author. I would take out my colored pens and write "Chapter One" on the top line with round, bubbly letters, alternating colors for every letter. *A masterful beginning.* Then I would choose the lucky color in which I would write this glorious novelette—a shade of blue-green. I would set the other pens aside, write the clichéd "Once upon a time," and then sit. And think. And think. And think. And then give up with a, "I could never write an entire book!" Then I would go eat lots of cheesy chips. *My fleshly cure to life's ailments.*

Writing was in me. It just wasn't ready to come out. Looking back, I now know that God planted a seed of desire for something He would one day bring about. It was a calling He had for me that, in time, after much watering and pruning and growing, He would make bloom.

I think of that story when I read this first line of Ephesians. Paul was an "apostle of Christ Jesus by the will of God." Years before, he would have never placed that title upon himself. In fact before becoming an apostle of Christ Jesus, Paul persecuted many Christians. He would have been on the Christian nightly news with a clandestine look on his face and the phrase "most wanted" stamped across the screen. He considered Christianity to be a cult—a group of rebellious Jews who needed punishing.

But Paul was an "apostle of Christ Jesus by the will of God."

When the time was right, Jesus showed himself to Paul. *Literally.* Paul (then called Saul) was on his way to Jerusalem to persecute more Christians when Jesus appeared in the sky. *Literally.* And He spoke to Paul. And Paul's world got rocked and shaken and turned upside down (see Acts 9). Paul was an "apostle of Christ Jesus by the will of God." And mark it down— we can't fight against the will of God. Well, we can. But we'll lose.

If God wills something, we can consider it done. The end. The word *will* in this verse means "a determination." God willed Paul to be an apostle of Christ Jesus—an ambassador of the gospel—not a tormenter of those who follow Him. And God made it happen.

That encourages me because it reminds me God has plans for His children. He does. He designed you and me to live in this exact period of time, with the exact family in which He placed us—warts and weird and wounds and all (see Psalm 139). He crafted us with a specific combination of gifts and talents and beauty no one else can imitate. His timing isn't always our timing, but He does have plans. And His plans for His children are good—in the eternal, He's-making-us-holy kind of way. He may not plan for us to change the course of Christendom like Paul did, but even in the seemingly mundane callings of our lives—the day-in-and-day-out of motherhood or daughter-hood or student-hood or wife-hood (I'm just making up all these "hoods")—God Almighty has a plan. And His plan can be trusted.

We may not always like or understand His plan. We may want to give it back to Him and say, "Um, no. Wrong plan, Jesus. Give me another plan that includes less hard stuff and more lattés." But He wills. And He wills good things for His children.

I know the temptation. It's tempting to say, "Well, I'm not Paul. And my life isn't that grand." But I lovingly shout this at your cute face, "Girlfriend, you're wrong!" You are a woman crafted by the hands of the Maker of heaven and earth. If you've come to the Father through faith in Christ then He willed it. You and I didn't make ourselves love Him. We didn't have the good idea one day to become "saved." We were graciously given eyes to see His love. He awakened us to His love. He willed us with His love. And in Christ, He calls you and me His "daughter."

By the will of God, we are His. It's called grace. And because we're His through the sacrifice of Christ, we now have peace with Him. "Grace to you and peace from God our Father and the Lord Jesus Christ" (Ephesians 1:2). As we walk through this letter written by the Apostle Paul, my prayer is that we would be wrecked by the matchless love of God. I pray He would overwhelm us with the depth and height and width of Christ's loving sacrifice. I hope we experience afresh His immeasurable love so we would be forever changed to love even the most unlovable people.

back to you
_____

In what ways has God gifted you? (It's OK to identify your strengths and gifts. They aren't from you. They're from Him! So rejoice.)

How has God strengthened or grown your gifts? How are you using your gifts to strengthen the faith of others (even those who are more difficult to love)? Or how do you think God may want you to use your gifts in the future?

Based upon today's text, how does God reveal His immeasurable love? (i.e. by calling us, by gifting us)

What one thing from today's study do you want to remember?

DAY TWO

Ephesians 1:3–6

As I mentioned yesterday, we'll start each day with prayer—asking God to open the eyes of our hearts that we might see Him through our time in His Word. Because remember: *dumb sheep*. After talking with Him, go ahead and dive into today's text with an expectant heart.

Today's text contains some difficult concepts. We'll read words like *predestined* and *chosen*. And those words can stir up lots of questions. But I pray when we get to the end of today's lesson, we have our hands raised high in praise of our God who cannot be fully explained or understood but who can be fully trusted. May our good Father God reveal Himself and His immeasurable love to us today.

Read Ephesians 1:3–6. Write these verses in your journal.

What does today's text reveal about God?

God the Father:

God the Son (Jesus Christ):

God the Holy Spirit:

What does today's text reveal about humankind?

God prompts: _____

I know me. I know what I'm capable of. I see the choices I make when I pursue my selfish desires. I can look back over my life at my outwardly rebellious college days documented through stacks of tear-stained journals, of which page after page reveals my youthful foolishness. Or I can (honestly) evaluate my *now* as a wife and a mom and all the impatience and unlove dwelling in me that the pressures of the every day reveal. No matter where I look on my timeline of life—every age, every season— each turn proves one overarching truth: when left to me, I'm a gigantic mess.

My natural self ain't got a redeeming quality about it. (That's "ain't" with all the Southern twang I can muster.) I'm self-protective, self-seeking, self-conscious, self . . . everything. But God! Paul tells us in the introduction of his letter to the Ephesians that the Father is to be praised because He has "blessed us in Christ with every spiritual blessing in the heavenly places" (Ephesians 1:3). I don't deserve "every spiritual blessing." I deserve a holy God's wrath with all its fury an enemy needs. Yet in sacrificial, immeasurable love, God the Father blesses rebellious humankind. God the Father blesses me.

Instead of soul death, Jesus gives new life. Instead of dirty rags, Christ clothes us with the righteousness of our spotless Lamb. Instead of being far from our Father—separated by the chasm of sin—we're brought near, into His throne room. We're fully accepted in the presence of our Maker because of Jesus' work on the Cross. It's scandalous.

Blessed be *Him* for not utterly forsaking us—for choosing us in Christ "before the foundation of the world" (v. 4).

I remember when I first sensed the Lord calling me. I sat under my daddy's preaching my whole, little life—every Sunday morning, Sunday night, and Wednesday night. Then as a nine-year-old girl, while sitting in the sanctuary during a good ol' Baptist revival, I sensed Jesus calling me to follow. "Follow Me, child. In Me alone is life." By His grace, I believed and walked to the front of that church, tears falling down my cheeks with a quiet confidence He had stirred. And even though I tried to suppress the voice of my Lord during my rebellious college days, the truth remained buried deep, "I'm His."

Blessed be the Father who chose us that we might see Jesus for who He is. That word *chose* in Greek means . . . chose. *You're welcome.* Later we read He "predestined" us, meaning God "determined before or ordained." I know it's a complicated, debated, hard-to-grasp issue, but God is God. There's a tension in which we as humans must live—a tension between God Almighty's sovereign control and our human free will. I don't claim to understand it. I just know He addresses both aspects in His Word. He awakens the spiritually dead *and* we choose this day whom we will serve. *Tension.* But He made this entire galaxy and every person on planet Earth. He set up the laws of nature and the plan of salvation. So He can do what He wants.

He could have left us to rot away in our sin, beginning with Adam and Eve and flowing down to all generations. But He loves His creation. He is love. And in His love and mercy, He decided not to leave us there in our sinful state. Beginning in those first pages of Scripture, we get a hint of the redemption to one day come in Christ. He chose a remnant of people—the Israelites—to be set apart from the rest of the world that they might know and love Him.

*The L*ORD *your God has chosen you to be a people for his treasured possession, out of all the peoples who are on the face of the earth. It was not because you were more in number than any other people that the L*ORD *set his love on you and chose you, for you were the fewest of all peoples, but it is because the L*ORD *loves you and is keeping the oath that he swore to your fathers.*

—DEUTERONOMY 7:6–8

He chose the Israelites. And if we have eyes to see and believe Jesus, it's because in His great grace He chose to open our eyes. He predestined us to be adopted as sons and daughters.

I know the questions. "Why me? Why isn't God 'choosing' to open the eyes of [fill in the blank]?" The answer: I don't know. I don't know why. I don't understand His timing. I don't grasp His ways. I don't know how His sovereignty and election and choosing and predestination all work together. But I know one thing. I know He alone is God. He doesn't answer to humankind. And when His ways confound us, we have to begin with what we know to be true and move forward from there.

We know that God is Father. He is the Creator. He is good, and He is doing good all the time. He sees the beginning from the end and everything in between. He has a plan. He hears and responds to the prayers of His people. He deeply loves and kindly moves. He's in absolute control. And it's not His desire that any perish. In His mercy He sent His Son Jesus to pay the penalty for our selfish sins. He put His wrath on the perfect Lamb—the wrath that should have fallen on you and me. And when we come to Him through faith in Jesus' death and Resurrection, we receive new life in Him. Then we go and tell others they too may be made new.

Dead people can't make themselves come to life. Blind people can't make themselves see. Deaf people can't make themselves hear. And that's us apart from Jesus—spiritually dead, blind, and deaf. Yet He chooses to reveal Himself to us. If we've been moved by His love and have chosen to follow Him, then it's because He opened our eyes. We no longer wear a cloak of shame. Instead we shout for joy at His work of love. Then in gratitude and urgency, we intercede for those around us who haven't yet seen Him for who He is. It's radical. It's unreasonable. It's complicated and perfectly simple all at the same time. It's love coming down and touching His creation: us.

Oh, Lord, let us never get over it.

_____ back to you

Spend a few minutes thinking through your own salvation story. What or who did the Father use to open your eyes to see Jesus for who He is—your Savior? What has your life been like since?

If God alone can awaken us to salvation, then why do you think He also instructs us to go and tell of Christ and to pray for one another?

What one thing from today's study do you want to remember?

DAY THREE

Ephesians 1:7–10

Spend a few minutes talking with the Lord. Voice the anxious places that tempt you to doubt God's faithfulness, and then remind your soul of His immeasurable love. I trust Him to graciously speak to each of us through His Word and by His Spirit today.

Read Ephesians 1:7–10. Write these verses in your journal.

What does today's text reveal about God?

> *God the Father:*

> *God the Son (Jesus Christ):*

> *God the Holy Spirit:*

What does today's text reveal about humankind?

God prompts:

Rain or shine, winter or summer, families flock to our state's indoor water park. Every once in a while, if we can pump ourselves up enough, we'll take our own family trip to that chlorine-saturated dome-o-fun. When you first walk into this park, after your eyes stop stinging from the chemical overload, you can't help but notice the humongous bucket hanging overhead. Over a period of time, water fills this gigantic bucket until it gets so full it topples over, spilling literally a thousand gallons of water on anyone standing within the 20-foot radius below. Sounds fun, huh? *It's not.* But that image came to my mind when I considered the words *riches* and *lavished* from today's portion of Paul's letter.

In Jesus, God has abundantly blessed us and forgiven us "according to the riches of his grace" (Ephesians 1:7). He abundantly lavishes. It's like He has taken a bucket bigger than we could ever measure and poured out His blessing on rebellious mankind. A blessing that would knock us down if we fully grasped its weight and splendor. But we don't get it. I don't get it. We get so consumed with things in this temporal world that the awe of the gospel gets lost in the hustle of life. Yet God doesn't stop loving His shortsighted children. In His great love, He set forth a plan to draw us to Himself through Christ. And He did it in the "fullness of time" (v. 10).

If there's anything that confounds us, it's the timing of God. I can't tell you how embarrassingly often I've sat before the Lord (of the universe) convinced it was time for such-and-such to happen. *Convinced.* "OK, Lord. It's time. Let's do this. Let's put this trial finally behind us. Enough is enough. Satan's had his say, but I'm all done. Come on, Lord. Come *on.*" As if I'm the coach pumping Him up for the big play of the game in which He's the star on the field.

It sounds ridiculous when I type it out. And it is.

Yes, we can ask God to do stuff and move mountains and heal bodies and change people. We can ask in faith, for He alone has the power. And sometimes, by His grace, He does immediately shake up our little worlds in response to the intercession of His people. But in the end, He's in charge. And just as Paul illustrates in this portion of Ephesians, God Almighty unfolds His plan according to His perfect timing.

When Jesus stepped into our timeline, He stepped in at the word of the Father. The Son breathed His first breath of oxygen exactly when and where the Father planned. That matters because it points to the sovereign rule of our God. He remains in complete control. Back when Adam and Eve sinned in that first garden, the plan rolled into motion—the plan of redemption through Christ's blood. It continued rolling through the pages of the Old Testament. It rolled through the New Testament. And the eternal plan of God's redemption of people continues to unfold today.

It's easy to look back at that great cloud of witnesses from Scripture and criticize their lack of faith in the sovereign rule of God. But when we're the ones walking in the middle of messy hours and painful weeks, we get blind and impatient. Our eyes settle down on this physical planet, and we grow convinced that somehow, someway we've fallen off God's radar. Because if we were indeed on His radar—we tell ourselves—then this mess would be cleaned up already. Things would change already. Healing would come already. Life would be easy already.

But lean in. I'm about to say something our souls too quickly forget. Something I'm going to say over and over because I need to hear it over and over. You ready?

God's in control, and His timing is perfect!

Pretend I shouted that in love with slightly crazed eyes. His timing was perfect when Jesus stepped onto this planet. And it's perfect now in our situations that test our patience and try our faith. There isn't a single person or situation that has fallen off His radar. And He knows what He's doing. And He does everything in love.

You and I have been placed in this exact space of time on purpose. We've been called to salvation with purpose. We've been crafted by Him and led into specific relationships on purpose. And just like one of my dear mentors recently said, "It isn't getting us to the 'promised land' that concerns God the most. It's who we'll be when we get there." *Mic drop.*

You and I are where we are, when we are, on purpose. And if God isn't changing things as fast as we think He should—ushering us into our proverbial promised lands—then it's because He has a reason. And more than likely, one of His thousands of reasons includes us being made more holy in the "not yet" and the "undone."

I don't say any of this lightly. We face tragic things. You may be walking through one of your most horrific personal storms. And if you and I were sitting face-to-face I'd weep with you, trusting fully that the Lord isn't calloused to your tears. He sees. He intimately cares. And at the very same time, He's in control.

Jesus came down to planet Earth at the exact right time. And He came with purpose. He came to gather His people to Himself because He loves us. He came to unite us rebels to the Father—us who have gone our own way, seeking life and pleasure in the creation rather than our good Creator. He lavished His abundant riches on man. Love came down to earth. May He root us deeper into His love today.

back to you

With what situation are you currently struggling to trust God's timing?

What truths could you meditate upon when you're tempted to doubt God's sovereign control?

What one thing from today's study do you want to remember?

DAY FOUR
Ephesians 1:11–14

Open your time by talking to your God for a few minutes. Yes, He blesses with tangible things at times. He blesses with protection or healing at times. But remember, *He's* the great reward. *He's* our ultimate gift. Thank Him for *Him*.

Read Ephesians 1:11–14. Write these verses in your journal.

What does today's text reveal about God?

God the Father:

God the Son (Jesus Christ):

God the Holy Spirit:

What does today's text reveal about humankind?

_____ God prompts:

In Jesus, we've obtained an inheritance from the Maker of heaven and earth. *Hello?! Seriously, y'all. That's amazing.* We grow complacent to the implications of our inheritance, but it's utterly amazing. Think about it. We're the prodigals. We're the people who seek after selfish gain and self-promotion and self-protection—in essence hating the beauty of God. Yet, in love the Father pursues us while we're floundering in our sin in order to heal us and forgive us. The Holy One who could rightly smite us instead graces us with an incorruptible inheritance.

Why does receiving an inheritance matter now, in this earthly life? It matters because God means for us to begin experiencing that inheritance now. Today. In the midst of our everyday relationships and everyday struggles, in the middle of political unrest and moral confusion, He intends for His kingdom to fill us and change us and spill out of us. That's not just theological talk. It's a spiritual reality. It's kingdom living. And kingdom living brings freedom—freedom from sin and freedom to love.

We then read in today's Ephesians text that in Christ we're "predestined according to [his] purpose" (Ephesians 1:11). I'm not going to linger here because Paul used that phrasing over and over in the introduction of this letter. And I hope by now thinking on that amazing, complex truth awes you and nearly sends you into the fetal position. *Not really. But really.* If we're His it's because He predestined it to happen. He chooses for His good pleasure. Amen. Hallelujah.

Next, we get to the word *all*, as in God works all things according to His will. Just as Paul says in Romans, "And we know that for those who love God all things work together for good, for those who are called according to his purpose" (Romans 8:28). That means if we are in Christ then whatever we're going through has, for reasons we may never fully comprehend, been allowed by our good Father. That doesn't mean that it will all *feel* good, but it will all *be* good—producing holy-good things.

I know we can have a hard time receiving that truth if we're in the midst of deep pain or significant loss. I know. But our feelings don't negate God's truths. And if—*when*—we find ourselves in those unbearable places, we grieve and writhe before God and then, by His strength, we wrestle our hearts back to places of truth. "You are good, God. And You're doing good. I can trust You."

From what Paul says, two things happen right before we're ushered into new life in Christ. We hear the gospel and then we believe. Some hear and don't believe. Some hear and think they believe. But others hear and truly believe.

Ultimately only God knows the heart of a person. But time will show fruit of the one who has truly believed. The Holy Spirit seals the believer and starts pressing out all the mess—aka sin—in us that steals from the life Christ died to give us. The word *sealed* means "to stamp (with a signet or private mark) for security or preservation." When we hear the gospel and believe, God seals us. He stamps us with His private mark. He comes to live inside us. He preserves us. We're His and therefore totally secure. He then starts to grow things in our lives like love, joy, peace, and patience (see Galatians 5:22–23).

I know that some shy away from Holy Spirit talk. But the value of the gift God gives us when He sends His Spirit to indwell us cannot be measured. Think about it. The Spirit of God Almighty—the One who formed worlds when He spoke—comes to live in me and in you

God gives His Spirit to us as a foretaste. The Spirit is a preview. One day we'll have our full inheritance that comes with Christ. No more sickness. No more tears. No more flesh. No more struggle. There will only be worship and freedom and love and perfect joy in the presence of our Savior. But until we fully realize our complete inheritance in Christ in eternity, we have a guarantee of what's to come. We have God Himself making His home in us. He's the earnest money.

We recently went through the real estate hurdles of selling and buying our home. *First-world problem.* But in that process I learned a little about earnest money. In real estate, the buyer gives the seller some money to say, "Look. I'm serious about this. I'm buying your house. Here's some money to prove it." That money transfers from the buyer to the seller. If the buyer backs out, the seller still gets to keep the money. If the sale goes through, that money applies to the purchase of the property.

God says, "My Spirit is the earnest money. And I won't back out. This deal will go through. And when it does, you'll receive your full inheritance." Until we meet Jesus in eternity, we walk around on planet Earth with God living in us. His Spirit wants to empower us, transform us, guide us, and be *big* in us as we walk out the days He ordains for us. But just because we're sealed with His Spirit doesn't mean we're always *filled* with His Spirit. We'll talk more about that later in the study. For now, however, rejoice in the fact that we have an inheritance from God Almighty marked by His Spirit coming to make His home in us who believe. What a gift. What love.

back to you
_____

How would you describe "kingdom living"?

How does the truth that God Himself seals you—comes to live inside of you—encourage you?

What one thing from today's study do you want to remember?

DAY FIVE
_____
Ephesians 1:15–19*a*

You probably have the hang of it now, but just as a reminder, take a few minutes to talk to God before diving into His Word. Expect Him to speak to those anxious places that plague your heart.

Read Ephesians 1:15–19a. Write these verses in your journal.

What does today's text reveal about God?

> *God the Father:*

> *God the Son (Jesus Christ):*

> *God the Holy Spirit:*

What does today's text reveal about humankind?

God prompts:

Faith and love. The two can't help but intertwine. As we have faith in the character and work of Jesus, the natural overflow will be love for God's people. We can't manufacture that kind of love. We can't manipulate that kind of love. It's a love that faith births and beckons.

When God brought me back to Himself after my rebellious college years, I remember my first experience with that kind of unmanufactured love for His people. I was at an outdoor Christian concert with a fairly new friend. And as I looked around that concert at all the people praising Jesus, I told her—loudly over the music—"I LOVE CHRISTIANS!" She couldn't really hear me so she thought I said, "I LOVE *CHRISTIAN!*" Which made the next few minutes a little awkward because we knew a guy named Christian, and loudly declaring my supposed love for him at that particular moment would have been very weird. We cleared it up. Anyway . . . faith in Jesus births love for His people. The two can't be separated.

Paul tells us he had heard of the Ephesians' "faith in the Lord Jesus" and "love toward all the saints" and that knowledge sparked thanksgiving and prayer in him (Ephesians 1:15–16). When we hear of or see another's faith and love being worked out in everyday life, it produces courage in us to press on. It inspires endurance. It's like when I go for a run. If I'm running alone, I may stop a few times to walk because I feel like I might die. But if I run with a friend or see a runner along the way, I'm inspired to keep going . . . even though my reasons are sometimes prideful. *God's still working on me.* But still, we humans affect one another. The faith of another can ignite our own faith. It's how God designed us. He designed us to walk out this life in community.

In his prayer, Paul asked God for something really huge. He asked the "Father of glory" to give the Ephesians the "Spirit of wisdom and revelation in the knowledge of him" (v. 17). Only the Father can give humankind a life-changing understanding of Himself. No amount of theological study, no amount of philosophical pondering, no amount of human effort can give us what Paul asked for in this text. Only God can grace us with heart-level knowledge of Himself. And He does it through His indwelling Spirit. When we, by His gracious revelation, begin to scratch the surface of knowledge of the Holy One, our perspective of everything changes. But Paul doesn't stop there.

When we have knowledge of God through the revelation of His Spirit, Paul tells us our hearts are enlightened. And it isn't until God enlightens our hearts—or gives them sight—that we will ever grasp the hope found in Christ. Oh, we can go to church. We can mentally grasp what Jesus did. But truly grasping the hope found in Jesus remains a gift of grace.

So what is our hope in Christ? *Great question. I'm so glad you asked.* It's trading God's wrath for His blessing. It's inheriting eternal life with Him instead of the crushing punishment of separation from our good Maker. It's beauty instead of ashes. It's His immeasurable power equipping us to overcome our many foes. Paul requested a priceless gift for the Ephesians. And his intercession for this group of people teaches us a number of profound realities about prayer. I'll just mention two.

First, prayer for spiritual understanding trumps prayer for physical well-being. I'm sure the Ephesians at this time in church history could have used some prayer for their physical well-being. This letter was most likely written in the middle of Nero's reign over the Roman Empire. And if you know anything about Nero, you know he was a vicious leader who hated Christians and proved it with his brutal executions of Jesus-followers. So the physical well-being of the Ephesians would have definitely been in question. Yet Paul didn't beg, "God, keep them safe! Don't let them get hurt." Instead Paul beseeched, "God, grace them with greater understanding of You!"

When praying for the people we love, it's easy to fall into the "keep them safe" or "heal their body" camp. And those prayers aren't bad prayers. God is the Defender and Healer. And we can ask Him to defend and heal. But Paul's prayer reminds me of the greater stakes. More than physical well-being, Paul prayed for spiritual understanding. In doing so, he jolts my own prayer life awake. His prayer causes me to evaluate my most urgent prayers for the people I love. It makes me ask whether my focus is physical or spiritual. The absolute greatest need of the people in my life is to have knowledge of the Father of glory. Everything else comes second (or third . . . or eighteenth).

Second, prayer calls forth God's kingdom in the lives of believers. We've talked about the sovereignty and predestination of God a number of times in the first few days of this study. And those are complicated truths about our God. But even though He sovereignly reigns, it seems He uses the prayers of His people as a catalyst for change on earth. Through prayer, His kingdom comes. When Jesus walked on this planet, He taught His disciples how to pray. He prioritized prayer. And the Father moved in response to His Son's prayers.

We too are given the gift and responsibility of prayer. We too can call forth spiritual understanding in the lives of believers. And there may be times when God waits to hear our words before He moves. Why? Well, because prayer is relationship. It's communication with the One who loves and satisfies us. And as we dance the dance of relationship with Him, prayers for others to experience Him in a deeper way overflow from our lips.

God can do whatever He wants whenever He wants. But in grace, we see in the Word that He sometimes chooses to do things in this created world simply because His children ask. I can't explain how that choice to answer prayer perfectly mingles with His sovereign reign. But I believe that scripturally we can affirm both . . . and then fall on our knees in utter awe of His complexity.

May He give you the Spirit of wisdom and revelation in the knowledge of Himself today. Amen.

_____ back to you

How has seeing or hearing of someone else's faith spurred you on in your own faith journey?

What do you most often pray for the people you love?

Spend some time praying Paul's prayer for the people you love.

What one thing from today's study do you want to remember?

_____ DAY SIX

Ephesians 1:19*b*–23

Begin your time by worshipping our good God through prayer. Spending time with Him isn't something to check off our list. Rather, it's an invitation to know and receive the love of our Maker.

Read Ephesians 1:19b–23. Write these verses in your journal.

What does today's text reveal about God?

God the Father:

God the Son (Jesus Christ):

God the Holy Spirit:

What does today's text reveal about humankind?

God prompts: _____

This portion of the text continues from yesterday's reading. We pick up mid-thought. So as a reminder, Paul told the Ephesians how he prays for them. He prays they would have the Spirit of wisdom and revelation and that they would know "the immeasurable greatness of his power toward us who believe, according to the working of [God's] great might" (Ephesians 1:19). In other words, Paul reiterates that the answer to his prayers will only come by the working of God's great might in and through God's people.

We hear it preached, "The same power that raised J‹ from the dead lives in you who believe in Jesus as Lord and Savior!" And we shout amen. But too often our amens dissolve when real life hits us in the face. We know that the Spirit of God resides inside us, ready and willing to empower us and reveal God's glory to and through us, but we can momentarily forget the implications of that profound truth. Paul reminds us. The same power that worked in Christ works in us. And when we face struggles and trials in this broken world, His Spirit can grace us with wisdom and understanding. His Spirit can remind us of who He is and who we are because of Jesus. His Spirit can strengthen us with a deep knowledge of the joy and hope available to us even on this often-treacherous journey.

Joy and hope. Sometimes the two seem so far out of reach, don't they?

Much of the struggle for joy and hope is fought on the battlefield of the mind. We so quickly forget who God is and what He promises. We forget who we are in Him. The suffering of this world steals our focus, and we need reminding. Jesus Christ sits at the right hand of the Father in the heavenly realm. The One who made heaven and earth, the One who died and rose for my salvation, the One who makes continual intercession on my behalf, sits on His throne in the heavenlies. That's not a fake world. It's not an mythical throne. It's a real place that we as humans can only barely imagine. Right now, Jesus sits at the right hand of the Father. He's in His resurrected body. All powers, seen and unseen, are subject to Him. And He holds all things together. *Yes, amen, hallelujah, praise the Lord.* But we forget.

The diagnosis comes. That person betrays. Our child rebels. Life takes our breath away. And we forget. We forget where Jesus sits. We forget He holds all power. We forget that He's in a real, live realm holding everything together, including our little lives. When the happenings of this world shake us up, we need reminding. We need the Spirit of God to lift our weary souls with the unchangeable reality of Jesus' position over and above all powers of the enemy. We need Him to strengthen us with the reminder of who we are in Him.

We, the church, are His body.

In that first garden, Adam and Eve reflected a spiritual reality that would one day come in Christ. Just as Adam and Eve were one flesh in the marital union, so the Bible teaches that we who've been adopted and redeemed are one with our Lord. We are His body. We are His bride.

Our broken world has tainted the beauty of this union. We're adulterous and promiscuous. Our eyes linger down here on planet Earth for satisfaction that can only be found in our Maker—the Lover of our souls. I know I've been adulterous to my Lord more times than I can count. Throughout my life I've looked for soul fullness in physical things or physical people, in essence turning my back on the One that satisfies. It disgusts me. The bent of my natural self is to betray the One who graciously pursues me in spite of me.

Thankfully, in His mercy, He hasn't forsaken me. The last (nearly) two decades of walking this life with Him have been a time of sweetness and growth. I still fail all the time. I'm still tempted to reject Him for my earthly comfort. But in His grace, He continues to draw me closer and closer into His infinite depths. He continues to teach me the glory of being His bride.

He's the faithful husband. He's kind and pursuing. He listens and comforts. He doesn't demand and list our failures. He draws us close and fans into flame the dreams and gifts He has placed in us. Yes, He allows us to walk through difficult and sometimes excruciating circumstances. But, for those who love

Him, He only allows that which will lead to our eternal good and His great glory. He only allows that which can produce in us the things we couldn't produce on our own. When life smacks us in the face, we have to purposefully remember. We, the church, are His body. He cares for His body. He tends to His body with a love immeasurable, even when we can't quite trace His hand.

back to you

Knowing we are Christ's body or bride, what other encouraging truths about Him can we stand upon when life gets difficult?

Think of the most challenging circumstance you currently face. Then fill in the blank below, allowing this truth to lead you into a prayer of trust and thanksgiving:

Father, you have placed Jesus above and beyond and in charge of all things. There is nothing out of His reach or care, not even _____ .
Once again today I declare my trust in You. Guide me. Grace me with wisdom. Empower me to walk faithful to Your precepts in the midst of this difficult circumstance.

What one thing from today's study do you want to remember?

week two

Irrational Love

Ephesians 2

DAY ONE

Ephesians 2:1–4

Well, we have one week of our study and one chapter of Ephesians officially behind us. I pray that God used it to grace you with a glimpse of His immeasurable love. This week we head into Ephesians 2, looking at God's irrational love—irrational because from an earthly perspective, His love makes absolutely no reasonable sense. It would have been reasonable for God to demolish us. But He didn't do that. Instead, His irrational love came down to make us alive. Spend a couple of minutes in prayer, and then head into today's text. I pray He graciously rocks our little worlds.

Read Ephesians 2:1–4. Write these verses in your journal.

What does today's text reveal about God?

God the Father:

God the Son (Jesus Christ):

God the Holy Spirit:

What does today's text reveal about humankind?

God prompts:

Today's text includes the super depressing side of our identity coin, which is why I included verse 4 in today's reading. Basically Paul tells us who we were before coming to faith in Jesus. Dead. Disobedient. Children of wrath. *Bad news first. Good news second.*

Paul explains that we were dead in our sin. Dead means dead. Spiritually un-alive. Yes, we physically moved around on this earth—breathing air, having conversations, doing jobs. But spiritually we were dead. And dead people can't come to life. Dead people don't climb out of graves. Dead people are just . . . dead.

In that spiritual deadness we were walking around in our sins. We were naturally following after the ways of this world. It's what we do in our spiritually dead state. We do whatever our flesh has impulse to do. We follow the "prince of the power of the air" (v. 2), aka Satan.

God created us to follow. Therefore all of us follow someone or something. And Paul's words imply there are two fundamental choices when it comes to following. In every moment of the day, we're either following God or following His enemy. There's no in-between. In our deadness, we were following Satan. And spiritual deadness exempts no one. Every human born on planet Earth follows the enemy of God. Rebellion saturates every human heart. It's our natural state.

Paul further explains that the spirit of the enemy works in "sons of disobedience" (v. 2). The enemy is at work. I grow numb to that reality. I grow numb to the spiritual war waging all around us. I get comfortable in this tangible world thinking about tangible things, forgetting that the enemy continually works, day in and day out. And do you know what he's doing? He's stealing.

If we're in Christ then the enemy can't steal our identity. We're the Lord's treasured possession. God adopts us as His children, declaring us heirs. The enemy can't change that. But he absolutely works continually to steal our focus. He works to steal our joy. He works to steal our peace. He works to steal our hope.

How? He lies. (We'll talk more about this in week six of our study. By then, we'll need reminding. But just to give you a taste of what's to come . . .)

In the Book of John, Jesus tells us that the devil "was a murderer from the beginning, and does not stand in the truth, because there is no truth in him. When he lies, he speaks out of his own character, for he is a liar and the father of lies" (8:44). The enemy works to steal our peace and joy and hope by lying to us all the time. Lie after lie after lie after lie. He lies about who God is. He lies about who we are in Jesus. He lies about what God has or hasn't promised. He lies. And we believe him.

We don't *want* to believe him. We really don't even mean to believe him. But his lies sound so similar to truth, and they always affirm our (volatile, often-irrational) feelings. So we take the bait. In no time, we're thinking on his lies.

What we think affects how we feel. What we think affects what we say and do. What we think affects the trajectory of our day. What we think affects the tone of our voice—*ahem*—which affects the people around us, which affects the people around them, and on and on it goes. That's why the enemy works to fill our minds with lies.

Years ago God dramatically convicted me of my thought life. I grew up as a "good" Southern Baptist preacher's kid and had learned over the years how to put on a "good" external show for the church folk. But inwardly I was a total mess. Insecurity and criticisms saturated my mind. I craved the approval of man. And the internal defeat led to years of running away from the Lord, seeking life in "sex, drugs, and rock 'n roll." It wasn't pretty.

After God graciously transformed my life, gave me a new heart, and awakened my love for Him, I started to realize the war waging in my mind. I became aware of the insecure thoughts lingering in the background of nearly every interaction. But it wasn't until my marriage went through significant crisis—when I wanted to point the finger in blame—that God dramatically convicted me of my thought life.

He tenderly showed me the critical thoughts that consumed my mind. He started unveiling the lies I harbored about my husband, myself, and my God. He graced me with fresh awareness of my internal meditations. And honestly, the revelation crushed me. The weight of my lie-saturated thought life humbled me. And God started me on a journey of learning how to take my thoughts captive to what's true, one thought at a time.

The enemy lies. He lies ruthlessly and continually. And before coming to faith in Jesus, we were slaves to his lies. Thankfully in Christ we've been empowered to first become aware of our thoughts and then take each thought captive to truth—following Jesus, rather than His enemy.

Before Christ, we were dead, disobedient, children of wrath. We were hopeless, deceived, and deserving of eternal separation from the holy God of the universe.

"But God . . ." *The good news.*

That's the super-amazing side of our identity coin in Christ. In spite of who we were apart from Jesus, God the Father shined hope and light onto our dark hearts. Love came down.

We're saving the rest of the good news for tomorrow. But as for today, I pray that the reality of our depravity apart from Jesus makes the glory of our redemption and the depth of His love that much more amazing.

back to you

Write out a short note of thanksgiving to God in response to today's text.

Give an example of how your thought life has affected your emotions or decisions.

What one thing from today's study do you want to remember?

DAY TWO

Ephesians 2:4–7

Yesterday's text presented the depravity of our natural humanity. Not a happy thing. Today, however, we get to see our glorious destiny in Jesus. Seriously, God does wild things. He does things that make no sense, like loving and saving His enemies—loving and saving us. Spend a few minutes in prayer asking God to prepare your heart for today's words of truth.

Read Ephesians 2:4–7. Write these verses in your journal.

What does today's text reveal about God?

   God the Father:

   God the Son (Jesus Christ):

   God the Holy Spirit:

What does today's text reveal about humankind?

God prompts:

If today's text doesn't excite us, then we need God to awaken our souls because today's verses declare the whole point of Christianity. Today's text, coupled with yesterday's text, is why we praise Jesus. It's why we worship on Sundays. It's why people give their lives to be martyred. It's why people go to prison in His name. It's why the Jesus movement hasn't ceased even after 2,000 years.

   Two words. "But God."

In spite of who we are apart from Him, in spite of our rebellion, in spite of our selfishness, in spite of our betrayal, in spite of our hatred of God, He miraculously chooses to make us alive. It's called mercy. He could have destroyed us. He had every reason. And yet, because He is rich in mercy, He relented.

The Greek word for *mercy* means "of uncertain affinity; compassion." I had to look up the word *affinity* because I must have purged all SAT words from my brain. Affinity means "sympathy marked by community of interest; an attraction to or liking for something." Verse 4 says that God is "rich in mercy" or affinity. He's abounding with sympathy and compassion for His people. And when I think about the whole of God's character as revealed through Jesus, it's clear that His compassion is more than feeling sorry for us humans—more than "bless their hearts, they're such idiots." I really believe that God not only loves us, He likes us. He doesn't always like what we do or what we think. He doesn't like sin and rebellion. But I'm certain there's a general liking of His children. He likes watching us become who He intends us to be. He likes seeing us discover our gifts and walk out His plans for our lives. No, we're not going to do it perfectly. We're going to fumble and fail. But I'm certain; He likes His kids.

If you're a parent (or even play a parental or mentoring role in someone's life), then may we follow His lead. Those that follow us, like our children, need to know we like them. They need to know that, yes, we love them, but we also *like* them. They crave to know that they make us smile just because of who they are. I think of that a lot . . . usually after failing to show my own children that I like them. By God's grace He jolts me awake, and I try to remind them of how much I like them by looking into their eyes when they talk or laughing at their made-up jokes or listening to them explain their favorite video game or dote on their hamster. Sure, they do dumb stuff in their immaturity at times. *Often.* But they desperately desire to know that I like them, simply because of who they are.

And you know what? We're just bigger and older versions of children. Maybe we know more stuff and shave our hairs and drive motor vehicles, but deep down we're still the same. We still crave to know that we're liked. And God richly likes us. He likes you. He likes me. He likes the quirks we have. He likes to see us do the things He created us to do. He likes to spend time with us. He doesn't get irritated when we say the same thing over and over again. He may know a better, more abundant way for us to live. He may want to purge things from us that steal the joy He has for us, but He still likes us. And He smiles over us. In spite of our rebellion, God our Father abounds with affinity for His children.

Out of His great love for us, even when we were dead, he "made us alive together with Christ" (Ephesians 2:5). Or in the words of the King James, He "hath quickened us together with Christ," which means He makes us "able to respond immediately to spiritual stimuli." So get this. God spiritually joins us to Christ to make us alive. God spiritually raises us from the dead with Jesus. And God then spiritually seats us with Jesus in His throne room. Like, for real. *He* does the work of salvation.

This isn't a theoretical concept. This is a spiritual reality for those who have come to faith in Jesus. We are joined with and reanimated to life with, and because of, Jesus. If not for Jesus, we'd still be spiritually in the grave.

What's even crazier is that His love doesn't stop there. It doesn't stop with salvation in the now. His love includes eternity. He says He does all of this positional transformation—saving us and seating us with Jesus—so that for all eternity He can show us the "immeasurable riches of his grace in kindness toward us in Christ Jesus" (v. 7). All eternity. Immeasurable riches. Grace in kindness. His love moves past human reason into this realm of lavishness for which our human scales don't even have a category. His love came down and obliterated our strings-attached, self-gratifying definition of love. It's truly awesome.

You are loved. You are liked. If you've come to faith in Jesus, you're seated with Him in the throne room of the living God, fully accepted and pleasing to Him. Breathe it in, friend.

back to you
_____

Do you struggle to believe that God likes you? If so, why?

How would remembering your spiritual position with the risen Jesus—seated with Him in the heavenlies—change the way you view your earthly struggles?

What one thing from today's reading do you want to remember?

DAY THREE
_____

Ephesians 2:8–10

Today's text may be familiar to you. And familiarity can be comforting. It's terrain we've walked. These are words we've read.

These are concepts we've memorized. But familiarity can also be disabling. We can become so familiar with words that they no longer impact our hearts. So today, ask God to grace you with fresh eyes for these familiar words.

Read Ephesians 2:8–10. Write these verses in your journal.

What does today's text reveal about God?

God the Father:

God the Son (Jesus Christ):

God the Holy Spirit:

What does today's text reveal about humankind?

God prompts:

My oldest child is a girl. And, I know I'm biased, but she's precious. She's kind. She's smart. She's artistic. She's tender to the hurting. She's gracious to her (often destructive and typically wild) brothers. She's just "good." But because of her natural "goodness," I recently started to wonder if she really grasped that Jesus saved her by grace. I started to wonder if her young teen soul really understood that beneath her more natural bent toward obedience lay a depraved heart, needy for the grace of a holy God. So I asked her Savior to show her. I asked Him to open her eyes to the sin that lurked in her heart beneath the good deeds of her flesh. And He did.

Over time, He allowed her to see her own sin to the point that one day she came to me and said, "Mom, sometimes I don't feel like I can worship God when we sing at church. I don't feel like I deserve to worship Him." I grabbed her up in my arms as if she were still small and said, "Baby girl, that's the point! That's the grace we sing about! Jesus saves us and calls us holy and righteous in spite of you and me. He saves us and brings us near the Father because of His blood sacrifice, not because of anything you or I could ever do."

Paul tells us, "By grace you have been saved through faith. And this is not your own doing; it is the gift of God, not a result of works, so that no one may boast" (Ephesians 2:8–9). Salvation. Is. Not. Our. Doing. Part of us just doesn't like this aspect of salvation. We want to think we've done something to earn it. Or we at least want to think we can do something to pay back the debt. But salvation is a gift from the God who owns and rules everything. We only receive this scandalous salvation by grace through faith. We can't do, say, or make anything to earn it.

Taken a step further, even the faith to believe is a work of the Spirit of God. We've looked at this before in Ephesians 1. But as a reminder, dead people cannot rise from the dead. They have to be beckoned to life by the Life Giver. Even the faith to believe in the Jesus who died for our sins erupts from the Spirit of God moving in the sinner's heart. Jesus said to the crowds in John 6, "This is the work of God, that you believe in him who he has sent" (v. 29). And later in the chapter, "All [of my followers] that the Father gives me will come to me, and whoever comes to me I will never cast out" (v. 37). And then later to some of His grumbling disciples, "There are some of you who do not believe . . . this is why I told you that no one can come to me unless it is granted him by the Father" (vv. 64–65).

I don't want to beat the same drum, but when we get to verses like these that confound us, we simply have to raise our hands and say, "God, You're crazy big. I don't understand why You do what You do. But I know You are good, and I know You can be fully trusted. So I simply praise You with all my heart that You chose to grace me with faith. And I ask that You would open the eyes of those I love who haven't yet believed unto salvation. Draw them to Yourself, Lord God."

If we had anything to do with our salvation, we could boast. We could gloat. And you know we would because we're human. We love to talk about how awesome we are. We love to talk about all of our accomplishments. But we can't claim an ounce or a speck of salvation as our own doing. We are God's "workmanship," a word that in the Greek means "a product; a thing that is made." God makes us. We're His. We're His design in Christ Jesus. And He makes us, in Jesus, for good works.

The good works—the ones that can truly be characterized as good—happen as an overflow of Him working in us. He prepares the works for us to do. He plans them before we're even a thought. He knows them and shapes them, and once we're alive in Him, He inspires us to walk in them.

I know God has things for you to do. He has good works set aside for you and me to accomplish. And He wants us to know them and walk in them. But we often get it backward. We think of some cool idea and then tack on a prayer, "Lord, make this work out. Take care of all the details." But in simply asking for His stamp of approval, we get it backwards.

The only way to know the works God has for us to do is for us to first know Him. When we first seek Him—worshipping Him and loving Him—He then graces us with inspiration for the good works He has planned. He may give us a grand idea for something that feels way too big for us to accomplish. He likes doing ridiculously huge things through small people who take Him at His Word. Or He may quietly nudge us with desire to speak a word of hope in a moment with a neighbor. Big and small, He has things for us to do. And as we worship Him in the moments of our lives, He graces us with eyes that see and feet that follow.

Salvation is a gift of grace. Faith is a gift of grace. Works are a gift of grace. Everything is grace, my friend. His irrational love. May that reality cause an eruption of praise in our souls.

back to you

_____

Why do you think Paul makes a point over and over to say that we have nothing to do with our redemption?

What good works do you sense God leading you to walk in? If you aren't sure, that's OK. Write a prayer to God—praise Him for who He is, and tell Him that you trust He will show you the things He wants you to do.

What one thing from today's study do you want to remember?

Ephesians 2:11–13

Often when I sit down to have focused time with the Lord, I have to purposefully remember what has my soul feeling tangled up. I have to pause and let the anxieties or fears rise to the surface of my consciousness so I can lay them before my God. I have to. Otherwise they'll just simmer beneath the surface of my everyday life aiming to taint the peace that Jesus offers. So let's do that before we dive into the Word today. Let's remember what's tangling us up. And then let's lay it all before Him.

Read Ephesians 2:11–13. Write these verses in your journal.

What does today's text reveal about God?

God the Father:

God the Son (Jesus Christ):

God the Holy Spirit:

What does today's text reveal about humankind?

God prompts: _____

Yesterday we looked at the scandalous grace we're under in Christ. We can take zero credit for our salvation. Zilch. Then we get to the "therefore" in verse 11. Paul says "therefore" to point us back to the last few sentences. Paul tells us two times in two verses, because of the gracious redemption we have in Jesus, to remember. Remember who we were. Remember we were dead and separated from the living God. Remember . . . because we forget. We forget from where we came. We forget from what He saved us. We forget the judgment we deserved. And when we forget, we tend to legalistically judge others.

A few years ago God graciously rocked my little, churchy, judgmental heart. He opened my eyes to the stance I inwardly, quietly took toward certain people who I was called to purely love. I had spiritual amnesia. I had forgotten from how much God had redeemed me. And in my forgetfulness, I demanded of others something that I myself could never give: perfection.

Remembering that I was once alienated from my Maker because of my sin changed how I related to and saw the people around me. I was once separated from the Lover of my soul. I was a stranger to the covenant of promise. I had no hope and lived without God in this world. I was the college idiot who should have died from my plethora of foolish choices. I am the one who still struggles with ever-present sin—revealed when I yell at my kids or clinch my jaw when someone does something I don't like. That's me. When we forget our origins and our current struggles, we judge others with a standard to which we could never achieve.

Paul tells us to remember. Since the letter was originally written to Gentiles (anyone who wasn't an Israelite), he tells the readers to remember that externally, they/we were rejected of God. They were not God's chosen ones like the Israelites. They even had physical proof of their rejection in that they were the uncircumcised. For those of you who may need a refresher, back in the Old Testament, God chose Abraham to be the familial line from which His people would come.

And I will establish my covenant between me and you and your offspring after you throughout their generations for an everlasting covenant, to be God to you and to your offspring after you. . . . This is my covenant, which you shall keep, between me and you and your offspring after you: Every male among you shall be circumcised. . . . So shall my covenant be in your flesh an everlasting covenant.

—GENESIS 17:7–13

God does what He does with purpose. We don't always understand, but we can trust that He's good and has holy reasons for all His allowances. He told Abraham that the sign of the covenant between Him and His chosen people would be circumcision. It would be a practice that would totally set His people apart from the rest of the peoples on the face of the earth. Because who would choose to do that if not instructed by the God of the universe? I'm thinking no one. Paul reminded the Ephesians, "You are the uncircumcised."

Paul then goes on to describe what it means to be the uncircumcised of God. He says, "Remember that you were at that time separated from Christ, alienated . . . strangers . . . having no hope and without God in the world" (Ephesians 2:12).

Apart from Jesus, this life is, and forever will be, hopeless. Apart from Christ we stand condemned by a holy God. And every human, everywhere and for all time, senses the soul-hopelessness that separation from the Father brings, whether we admit it or not. In fact, hopelessness fuels the depression, anxiety, and fear that run rampant in the hearts of us all.

Hopelessness leads us to clamor for someone or something to ease the ache. And it only takes a cursory glance to see that our world grasps at hundreds of thousands of things to ease the ache that hopelessness leaves. We live addicted to drugs, sex, social media, shopping, and the approval of other fallen humans in efforts to fill the hole of our souls. I know because I have to continually guard my own heart, or I do the same.

Years ago I too blatantly grasped at worldly things to ease the hopelessness I sensed deep within. And looking back at those years, it's easy to see the selfish sin that ate away at my soul. But even now, two decades into my adventure with Jesus, I still find myself periodically grasping at people and things in this world to give me the peace and hope found ultimately in Jesus alone. I can grasp at good things, even holy things— like a godly marriage or children who follow after Jesus with abandon—to give me the soul-rest I crave. I momentarily forget that even though God gives good, holy gifts within this world, we're not meant to grasp at those gifts as our lifeline. We're to hold them with open hands—thankful and trusting that God is good, whether He gives them or takes them away.

Without a vibrant faith in Jesus, we live hopeless lives. We may have moments or seasons of happiness, but deep down we are strangers to the promises found in covenant with our Maker. We're alienated from our Father God. Apart from Christ we live without lasting hope.

But God. Again, His radical mercy overwhelms me.

"But now in Christ Jesus you who once were far off have been brought near by the blood of Christ" (v. 13). I was far, but now I'm near. That pretty much sums it up in a quick seven words. And it's such a tender bringing near. It reminds me of that rebellious prodigal who finally walks shamefully back home only to find his dad running toward him (see Luke 15:11-24). The father had been watching and waiting. And instead of shame, the father lavishes love. He embraces him. He receives him. He celebrates his repentance.

We too through the blood of Christ are brought near. We too when awakened to the beauty of Jesus—expressed through deep, heartfelt repentance for our sin—are spiritually brought near. No longer aliens in a foreign land, we're sons and daughters celebrated by the Father. May we remember. May we remember from where we came. May we remember the great grace we're under. May we remember how deep the Father's love is for us.

back to you

Share a time when you've seen forgetfulness of your own journey to salvation lead you to judging another in their journey.

What can we do to purposefully practice remembering who we were before Christ redeemed us?

What does hopelessness typically lead you to depend upon (other than the Lord)? Being able to identify our flesh response to hopelessness will help us fight future hopelessness when it arises.

What one thing from today's study do you want to remember?

DAY FIVE
Ephesians 2:14–18

Spend a couple of minutes in prayer, asking God to speak to your soul today. He sees you. He knows you. He is being faithful and good, even in the undone of today.

Read Ephesians 2:14–18. Write these verses in your journal.

What does today's text reveal about God?

God the Father:

God the Son (Jesus Christ):

God the Holy Spirit:

What does today's text reveal about humankind?

God Prompts:

In Ephesians 2:14–18, Paul refers to the dividing wall between the circumcised and the uncircumcised. The "wall of hostility" between those who are God's chosen people from the Old Testament—the Israelites—and those who were not—the Gentiles. Paul tells us there has been enmity and hatred between these two groups. And God has now brought peace through Christ by breaking down the wall, ushering in oneness and unity among all who follow Him

Have you ever sensed a wall of hostility between you and someone else? Maybe it's a wall based upon race or personal convictions (like in this text). Or maybe the wall was built as a reaction to circumstances that took place in a relationship. Either way, I think it's safe to say we've all had some experience building or facing walls of hostility at various times in our lives. I know from experience that we hurting people fortify those walls in efforts to protect our souls from future damage. I know. And I know that we justify the walls and think we need the walls to survive. But here's the problem with walls. Yes, they may keep our supposed enemies at a distance, but they can also distance us from our Healer.

For years I allowed tall walls to guard some personal pain in my own life from past hurts. I built huge walls around my heart because something in me believed that if I allowed God to heal my deepest wounds, the pain would have been purposeless. Deep down I believed healing would negate the suffering. But God tenderly ministers to His children.

One morning, I had a vision of sorts. An image appeared in my mind when I was praying. I saw a little girl hiding something in her hands. Then in my mind I saw a huge, kind, Fatherly hand reaching toward her, asking the girl to give Him what she was hiding. She reluctantly opened her hands and there was a heart—tattered, bandaged, and infected—desperately needing healing. I realized the little girl was me. And the hand was that of my Heavenly Father. The invitation was clear. He wanted me to allow Him entrance. He wanted to tear down the wall I had built around my pain. He wanted to bring healing and peace to an inner chaos that had simmered under the surface of my days. And slowly, over time, I welcomed Him into those hostile places. I asked Him to tear down the walls I had erected and usher in the peace only He could give.

I don't know what kind of walls you've built in your own life, but I do know this: the Heavenly Father can tear them down and bring healing to the most tender wounds and the most vile hatred. People can't do that. An apology can't do that. But God can. He can replace the chaos with peace. It may take time—most wounds heal slowly. But one day, and then the next and then the next, with hands and heart open to the Healer, peace will come. I know. Because He promises.

Through Christ, God broke the walls of hostility between the Israelites and the Gentiles. And He can do the same with us. We serve a God who desires unity among His people. Unity reflects His character. Discord does not.

I can hear the rebuttal now. "But it's not me that causes the discord. It's *them*. They won't live in unity with me. They keep hurting me. They are the problem." I get it. I understand. The struggle is real. But what if Jesus had said that about us? We'd still be enemies of God. Instead, He sacrificed Himself for those who hated Him. "Well, I'm not Jesus," says everyone everywhere. True. We're not. And people hurt us. Wounds happen. Walls are built. But *as much as it depends upon us*, the calling to unity remains—by the absolute grace of God through the power of His Spirit.

> *Repay no one evil for evil, but give thought to do what is honorable in the sight of all. If possible, so far as it depends on you, live peaceably with all. Beloved, never avenge yourselves, but leave it to the wrath of God, for it is written, "Vengeance is mine, I will repay, says the Lord." To the contrary, "if your enemy is hungry feed him; if he is thirsty, give him something to drink; for by so doing you will heap burning coals on his head." Do not be overcome by evil, but overcome evil with good.*
>
> —ROMANS 12:17–21

We live in a broken world. Painful things will happen. Until Jesus comes again, this earth and everyone in it groans for the Redeemer to return. People (we) will keep on doing things that cause others to crave revenge. But if we're truly following the One who died for us, then we follow Him while carrying our cross. We follow Him by laying down our self-life and trusting Him to be the judge.

The Father's love came down through the gracious work of Jesus, obliterating the walls of hostility that divide. May we welcome Him in.

back to you

Can you identify a wall of hostility in your own life (past and/or present)? If so, who is it toward and why?

If you do have a wall of hostility erected between you and another, I challenge you to ask God to tear it down and replace it with peace. It won't be easy. It will take time. But if you're up for it, write out a prayer of repentance and desire. Our God is trustworthy with our wounds.

What one thing from today's study do you want to remember?

DAY SIX

Ephesians 2:19–22

Yesterday we looked at how God's love obliterates walls of hostility. And if you're like me, that text brought conviction. Because if there's anything we want to protect it's our hurts and our walls. But God's love came down to transform all it touches. May His love touch our souls more deeply than we expect today.

Read Ephesians 2:19–22. Write these verses in your journal.

What does today's text reveal about God?

God the Father:

God the Son (Jesus Christ):

God the Holy Spirit:

What does today's text reveal about humankind?

God prompts:

Are. Paul says that once we're brought to the Father through Christ, we *are* fellow citizens and members of the household of God. No one can change who we are. No words spoken against us, no thoughts or feelings that take up space in our souls— nothing can change our identity. In Christ, we are God's family. It's done. The enemy knows he can't change who we are. He can only change our *perception* of who we are. That's a big difference. Paul reminded the Gentiles, "you are no longer strangers and aliens, but you are . . . members of the household of God" (Ephesians 2:19).

Not only does Paul affirm their identity, he addresses the heritage they receive. The Father not only brings them and us near, He also places us onto the foundation of the apostles and prophets. In essence He says, "This is your heritage." The prophets and apostles of centuries past become our history. Through faith in Christ, we stand upon a legacy of faith that goes all the way back to the beginning. And that's encouraging, especially for those who have at times felt like the outcast.

In Christ, we have a place. In Christ, we're fully accepted as His. In Christ, we're home.

It's good to get home, isn't it? Even with all of the messiness that often fills our earthly homes, arriving to that front door after a long trip proves to be especially satisfying.

Growing up my family traveled quite a bit. My mama worked for a major airline, so we explored the world on their dime. We accumulated lots of stories of our experiences, often to the embarrassment of one of our family members. Like the time when our waiter at a fancy Manhattan restaurant didn't understand our Southern twang and politely asked us to follow him . . . out the back door. Literally, he led us to the alley and closed the door, leaving us alone staring at one another like, "What in the world just happened?" Or the time we rushed into a German shop before catching a train, shouting at the clerk in efforts to find a pair of Birkenstocks that would fit us. Sidenote: shouting in English doesn't make Germans understand you any better. *Oh, I have many more stories. Let's do coffee some time.* But my point is, though traveling is fun and amazing and exciting, after a while you just want to get home.

Coming to Christ . . . well . . . isn't like my stories at all. But, coming to Christ is like coming home. We travel around this earth, searching for acceptance. Then Christ draws us to Himself and says, "Child, this is home. I'm your home." And in Him, we find we can breathe a huge sigh of relief, sit down, and cease the striving for acceptance.

Paul tells us, we are of the household of God Almighty. Our heritage is that of the prophets and apostles who went before us. But not only the apostles and prophets, Christ Himself is the cornerstone of our foundation.

I don't know much about construction. Yes, my husband and I periodically do house projects that include sledgehammers and pry bars. Well, he does projects. I watch and hand him tools while swiping through pictures I've saved for inspiration. But I do know a little about the cornerstone of a structure. The cornerstone is critical. It's the stone of the foundation used as the guide for the rest of the building. It's the starting place. From the cornerstone, everything else is laid.

Christ is called the cornerstone of our faith. He is the starting point. All the prophets and apostles of centuries past, even prior to Christ's earthly coming, were built upon Him. Everything points to Him. Everything is measured by and from Him. He's the point. And He—the chief cornerstone—came down to rescue us. Talk about a secure foundation.

In Christ "the whole structure, being joined together, grows into a holy temple in the Lord. In Him you also are being built together into a dwelling place for God by the Spirit" (vv. 21–22). In Christ—all of those who have walked before us by faith, plus you and me and everyone beside and coming behind us— we're all joined together. We're growing into a temple of the Lord. We, together, are a dwelling place for God by His Spirit.

You and I—if we've come by faith to Christ—have been individually gifted with the indwelling Holy Spirit. But the heart of God beckons us into community. He draws us into relationship. He dwells in the body of believers—from all nations and cultures—"built together into a dwelling place for God" (v. 22).

That's why we need one another. We need to be in relationship with one another. We need to glean from the gifts and experiences of one another. We weren't meant to do life singularly. We're designed to be in community. And not just in community with those who look like and talk like and worship like us. We're designed to be in community with those different from us, living out their faith in the beautiful diversity expressed by the Spirit of God Himself.

Love came down through Christ. Love came down to crush the dividing walls of hostility between humans and to build a unified body of believers, beautifully diverse in the Spirit of God for the glory of the King. Welcome home.

back to you
_____

Who does God say you are in Christ?

What truths can you rehearse the next time you're tempted to believe you're an outcast?

How does community with fellow believers encourage your own faith walk?

What one thing from today's study do you want to remember?

week three

Mysterious Love

Ephesians 3

DAY ONE

Ephesians 3:1–3

God sits above and beyond us, yet He's intimately involved in our little lives. He moves with eternity in mind, yet He sees our minutes. He deserves all praise, all the time, yet He graciously draws His enemies close. His love mystifies the human mind. His love goes beyond human reason. Today, as we open the Word, let's ask this magnificent God to reveal even more of His mysterious love to our finite hearts and minds. And then let's expect that He will.

Read Ephesians 3:1–3. Write these verses in your journal.

What does today's text reveal about God?

God the Father:

God the Son (Jesus Christ):

God the Holy Spirit:

What does today's text reveal about humankind?

God prompts:
_____

Ephesians 3 starts with the words "for this reason," reminding us that the original text wasn't broken up into chapters and verses. It was a continuous letter written to the Gentiles of the city of Ephesus. So we have to ask ourselves what reason Paul is referring to. And when we look back at that last sentence from Ephesians 2 we can remember that he's referring to the fact that God's people—Jew and Gentile—"are being built together into a dwelling place for God by His Spirit" (v. 22). Because we're being built together into a dwelling place, Paul says he's "a prisoner of Christ Jesus on behalf of you Gentiles" (3:1). Paul is a prisoner of Christ Jesus.

To be a prisoner is to be bound. Paul is bound to Christ. Not by force. Christ hasn't forced Paul to be captive to Him. The revelation that Paul received of Christ—the gospel message—has him bound. He can't help but remain captive.

It reminds me of that text in the Book of John when Jesus spoke some hard words and "many of his disciples turned back and no longer walked with him" (John 6:66). Then Jesus turned to His twelve disciples and asked if they wanted to leave too. And Peter answered, "Lord, to whom shall we go? You have the words of eternal life, and we have believed, and have come to know, that you are the Holy One of God" (vv. 68–69). Peter's like, "Jesus, we're bound. We can't leave You. Our beliefs won't let us." Similarly Paul was bound to Christ, not because Jesus wouldn't let him leave. Paul was bound because of what he now understood to be the ultimate reality of life. He couldn't help but remain a prisoner of His Savior.

Me? Sometimes I'd say I'm truly, deeply, honestly a prisoner of Christ. I want to be a prisoner to Jesus. That's my spirit's longing. But if I'm honest with myself, at times I see fear taking me captive. Or the approval of others tempting my allegiance. Or whether or not it's a good hair day driving my bondage. Thankfully, God remains patient with our process. And if we're truly His, then He's slowly transforming us to look more and more like Christ—freer and freer in Him.

Paul then pauses and goes into a long parenthetical in verses 2–13. I love Paul's parenthetical thoughts. He goes into a righteous tangent describing the stewardship given to him and the mystery of Christ made known to him by revelation. Remember the account of Paul's conversion from the Book of Acts? Paul—a highly accomplished and respected Jew—was on the road to Damascus when Jesus appeared to him. Jesus revealed His glory and His story to Paul, and Paul believed. He became captive to His gracious Savior. He became a steward of grace (see Acts 9:1–22).

On that road to Damascus, the Maker of heaven and earth could have rightly annihilated Paul and all his murderous intentions. He could have. But instead God gave grace. Instead God gave vision and revelation into the heavenlies so that Paul could see the glory of the Savior. This is the grace Paul would later steward.

To steward something is to manage or care for something that isn't one's own. It's like if someone says, "Here, lady, I'm going to give you a million dollars to steward for me. Let's see what you do with it." *People constantly want to give me millions of dollars to steward. It's getting annoying.* In this highly unlikely scenario, it's not my money. I'm just given management over it.

In Christ, Paul was given stewardship of God's grace. The grace is God's. Paul, having received this mysteriously scandalous grace, is then called to steward it. The way to steward something well is to do whatever one can do to cause that thing to accomplish its greatest purpose. To steward the million dollars well we would want to do things that would cause the money to grow. To steward the grace of God well means doing things to multiply it. And the way we multiply the grace of God is by sharing it with others that they would be transformed by the grace of God. Because when people are changed by the grace of God, then they tell others of the transforming grace of God, and on and on.

Paul stewarded the grace of God by sharing the grace of God with outcasts. He shared the grace of God with the very people his upbringing would have declared unclean—the Gentiles. And in doing so, God's grace spread.

But Paul isn't the only one called to steward the grace of God. If we've received Christ, then we too are given stewardship. We too have an invaluable treasure to give to those around us. We may not all be evangelists, traveling to foreign lands with a mere knapsack and sandals. But we're all gifted. We're artists and writers. We're students and baristas. We're moms and teachers. We're friends and sisters. We're doctors and politicians. *Here's where I deleted my joke about politicians not being stewards of God's grace because I know a couple of amazing politicians.* In Christ, we're stewards of the grace of God given to us. And we're to steward wherever and however He leads.

Paul, a prisoner and steward. Me, a prisoner and steward. You, a prisoner and steward. May we steward His matchless grace well.

back to you

All of us struggle at times by allowing our hearts to be captive to someone or something other than Christ. What would you say most often tempts your heart's allegiance from Christ?

Write out a prayer to the Lord declaring your desire to be prisoner to Him alone.

What does it look like to steward the grace of God in our lives?

What one thing from today's study do you want to remember?

DAY TWO

Ephesians 3:4–7

My prayer for us today is that we would have ears that hear our good God, eyes that see His faithful movement, and feet that follow His lead. Spend a few minutes asking Him for the same.

Read Ephesians 3:4–7. Write these verses in your journal.

What does today's text reveal about God?

    God the Father:

    God the Son (Jesus Christ):

    God the Holy Spirit:

What does today's text reveal about humankind?

God prompts:

A number of years ago, when God began my journey as an author, I questioned whether or not the world needed yet another voice. I mean, for real. It feels like every single person on the planet has a book or a blog or a podcast. Words and perspective saturate our culture. But I read *A Godward Life* by John Piper, and it gave me courage and conviction to press on with the call I sensed on my life. In it he said, "Generation after generation has read the insights of its writers. This is why fresh statements of old truth are always needed. Without them people will read error."

Words are power. Words can stir up faith and awaken a dream. Words can inspire us to keep running with eyes set on the Lord. Paul says to the Ephesians, "When you read this" (Ephesians 3:4). Paul wrote the truths God had revealed that they might have greater understanding of the mystery of Christ. And now, hundreds of years later, we too read the words that expound the mystery of Jesus. No, that's not the main point of the text, but we need reminding. We too have words to speak—words to write—that those walking beside us and coming behind us on this journey might be spurred on in their faith. Maybe you're called to write a book or start a podcast. Or maybe you're called to write notes of courage to a friend walking a difficult road. Either way, words hold power. God prompts us to use our words to minister Him into the lives of those around us.

The mystery to which Paul refers is the joining together of Jew and Gentile. Gentiles would become fellow heirs, grafted into the family of God by faith. God explained that His children are not children because of lineage; children are children of God because of faith in the work of Christ. Paul says the insight into this mystery is something new, something different from what God had revealed to generations past. But now, by His Spirit through the gospel, God has opened human eyes to this mystery of unity.

Let's look at both of these phrases: *by His Spirit* and *through the gospel*. First, it's only by the Spirit of God that we understand anything about God. Seriously. I know me. I've seen what I'm capable of when I'm not walking in fellowship with my Maker.

I see who I am when I don't heed the voice of God. *It isn't pretty.* And I know—both from Scripture and experience—that apart from Him giving me eyes to see Him, I would still be blind. Apart from Him gracing me with feet that quicken to obey His voice, I'd stay planted in my sin.

Consider a conversation between Jesus and His disciples, "'Who do you say that I am?' Simon Peter replied, 'You are the Christ, the Son of the living God.' And Jesus answered him, 'Blessed are you, Simon Bar-Jonah! For flesh and blood has not revealed this to you, but my Father who is in heaven'" (Matthew 16:15–17). The Father had revealed truth to Peter. The other disciples said Jesus was someone or something else, maybe even a reincarnate Elijah or Jeremiah. But Peter had been given divine knowledge. God had opened his eyes to truth. And that same pattern remains today. Apart from His initiation in our lives, we remain ignorant and in the dark. But by His Spirit, He reveals Himself. He graces us, mere humans, with glimpses of His plan. Paul, along with the other apostles and prophets, were graced with understanding by the Spirit of God.

That second phrase "through the gospel" refers to how Gentiles and Jews become one. Jesus, through His death and Resurrection, ushers in oneness. Jesus ushers in unity. It's through the gospel, not religion, that we're made right before the Father. It doesn't matter how outwardly religious we act. God Almighty looks at the heart. And unless the heart humbles itself and repents, it can't receive the mercy of a holy God. All humans, no matter the heritage or skin color or social status, need mercy. All of us stand condemned. And either we come under the punishment Christ took on our behalf or we have to take the punishment from our Maker. One way or another, God judges our sin.

Jew and Gentile, young and old, king and slave, all become heirs in the same way. We become heirs of God by God's Spirit through the gospel of Jesus Christ. Paul says it's this gospel of which he was made a minister. And if we're followers of Jesus, we too have a ministry. We too are called to proclaim Jesus to a needy world—beginning with those inside the walls of our home and then flowing out to the places and spaces He has us go in the daily-ness of life.

We have to remember the point of this life. I have to remember. The main thing on planet Earth is for us as children of God to receive the Father's love through Christ and then deliver the good news of Jesus to a lost world. Yes, we have groceries to buy and spilled milk to mop up and people to feed. Yes, the regular tasks of life keep demanding our attention. *Constantly.* But thumping beneath the surface of the mundane is a glorious truth. Jesus came to give us life. Jesus came to unite humans to the Father. May those truths be ever on our lips.

back to you
_____

How have the words of another spurred on your faith?

Is there someone in your life who needs some words that point them to the Lord? If so, what could you tell them? (Consider writing those truths in a note and dropping it in the mail.)

What can you do today to keep the main point in mind?

What one thing from today's study do you want to remember?

DAY THREE

Ephesians 3:8–10

Take a minute to verbalize to the Lord whatever has your heart tangled. Do fears lurk in your soul? Do worries plague your thought life? Lay them all before the Lord and then remind yourself of what's true. The Father intimately knows your every struggle. And He cares. He will guide. He will remain faithful.

Read Ephesians 3:8–10. Write these verses in your journal.

What does today's text reveal about God?

God the Father:

God the Son (Jesus Christ):

God the Holy Spirit:

What does today's text reveal about humankind?

God prompts: _____   _____

God crushed me a number of years ago in the most loving of ways. I had grown inwardly proud of my choices in a particular relationship where I'd been hurt. To the point that, though I would have never voiced it in a million years, I thought myself better than the other person. *Holier. Purer.* I thought real highly of how Christianly I could be—not reviling when reviled or cursing when cursed. But then God let me see. He let me fall into a deep pit of sin. I followed my sinful heart into a place of rebellion I would have never thought I'd walk. And when He exposed my sin to the people around me, I was utterly crushed. Seeing what I was capable of made me physically ill, emotionally devastated, and spiritually depressed.

I was certain I would never be in ministry again. I was sure this situation would be what disqualified me from ever being used of God in the future. But in time, as God slowly lifted me out of the ash heap, I realized He had done something purifying in me through this horrific exposure. He had given me a fuller glimpse of my depravity. He had brought me to the place where I could honestly say, "No, I'm way less worthy than you—all of you."

Paul called himself "the very least." He remembered who he was before Jesus appeared to him on that road to Damascus. He remembered that he called for the murder of Christ followers. He knew the depravity of his flesh. And knowing his own depravity made the grace of God that much more scandalous. It made the riches of Christ completely unsearchable.

I don't know who you have beef with. *Beef. I'm sure people don't say this anymore.* I have no statistical support, but I would guess that at the core of most of the complaints we have with others is our own pride. At the root, we simply think we know better in our difficult relationships. We think we have rights they aren't honoring. We have wounds to which they're not tending. But what if, *what if,* we dared to ask God to show us our own depravity? What if we got to the place where we truly, deeply, honestly believed ourselves to be the very least? I'm thinking that would reflect our Savior.

Paul continues. He—the very least—had been given the ministry of preaching this mystery of unity and forgiveness to the Gentiles "so that through the church the manifold wisdom of God might now be made known to the rulers and authorities in the heavenly places" (Ephesians 3:10). This sentence takes my breath away.

First, "through the church the manifold wisdom of God" is made known. The church isn't a physical building. The church is the body of Christ—the people of God. When we come to the Father through faith in Christ, He adopts us as His own. He makes His home *in* us. And we become the temple of the Holy God, as recorded in 1 Corinthians 3:16, "Do you not know that you are God's temple and that God's Spirit dwells in you?" It's wild, but it's what He does.

I'm not going to belabor this next point because I've mentioned it before, but as the body of Christ, we need to be in fellowship with one another. You and I need to be in a local church, living real life beside other Christ followers. Yes, the church at large makes lots and lots of poor choices at times. Remember, the church is made up of humans. And humans . . . well . . . are human. But mess and all, we need one another. So if you aren't in a local gathering of believers, I would encourage you to start looking and praying for God to show you a local group of Bible-believing, Spirit-filled Christians you can do life beside. And if you are in a local church, then I would encourage you (as I preach to myself) to live authentically with a handful of Jesus-seeking people. We need it. We need authenticity. We need the body of Christ to spur us on. It's "through the church" that God is made known.

Second, this multifaceted, immeasurable wisdom of God is made known through the church "to the rulers and authorities in the heavenly places." *What?!* Rulers and authorities in the heavenly places! Through you and me—the body of Christ— the wisdom of God, seen in the gospel of Christ, is made known to the spirit world. We'll read more about the unseen world later in this letter to the Ephesians. But for now Paul tells us that our ministering of the truth of God throughout the earth actually affects the unseen world. I don't claim to understand what he exactly means by that. But I know it's true. And I know we forget.

We forget that a heavenly war continually wages. We forget while we're sipping our vanilla latte or attending to our child or scrolling through Facebook that there's a spiritual realm and we can have an effect upon it.

The mysterious love of God came down through Christ. It came down and miraculously transforms humankind. It transforms murderers into missionaries. It transforms adulterers into faithful worshippers. The love of God transforms you and me into the hands and feet of Christ that we might make known the manifold wisdom of God Almighty to those seen *and* unseen.

_____ back to you

Who do you tend to think of yourself to be better than?

If God brought someone to mind, I double-dog dare you to write a prayer asking God to reveal your own depravity. God opposes the proud but gives grace to the humble.

What could you do this week to become even more connected and authentic with a local group of Jesus followers?

What one thing from today's reading do you want to remember?

_____ DAY FOUR
Ephesians 3:11–13

Today we touch on some of the holy purposes for suffering. These purposes don't make suffering easier in the moment. Suffering hurts. It's complex and unwanted. But remembering what's true about our God helps us to keep perspective when suffering knocks on our door. Spend a few minutes asking God to prepare your heart for His Word today. Then dive in.

Read Ephesians 3:11–13. Write these verses in your journal.

What does today's text reveal about God?

    God the Father:

    God the Son (Jesus Christ):

    God the Holy Spirit:

What does today's text reveal about humankind?

God prompts: _____

God never had a plan B. Back in the Garden of Eden, when God spoke everything into existence, the plan always included Jesus, the coming Redeemer. Always. He designed humans with the capacity to love Him. But in order to have the capacity to love and adore, mankind must also have the capacity to hate and rebel. And hate and rebel is what humans naturally choose. We choose rebellion until we finally see that rebellion equals death.

From all eternity, God's manifold wisdom included Christ Jesus. Why does that matter now? Because it reminds us that God has a plan. Nothing catches Him off guard. He doesn't ever sit on His holy throne and say, "*Wow!* I didn't see that coming!"—not in that garden of old and not in our lives today. Nothing happens without going through His eternal hands of loving purpose. If He allows something into the life of one of His children, then He allows it on purpose. We may not know why. We may never know why. And we may kick and scream in disagreement for a minute (or for months). But God does things on purpose. And He can be fully trusted.

Paul reminds us that God's eternal plan included Christ Jesus. God's plan included the perfect, Holy Son stepping into time on planet Earth. The Father's plan included the Son being rejected, beaten, stripped of His human clothes, nailed to a shameful Cross, and ultimately bearing the wrath of God for the sins of mankind. His plan included the crucified Messiah. But that grave couldn't hold the Lord God. He overcame sin and death when He stood and walked out of the tomb. And it's through faith in the resurrected Christ that we—once enemies of God—have "boldness and access with confidence" to the Father (Ephesians 3:12).

Growing up I wasn't bold at all. I was always the smallest girl in my class. I had big, thick glasses and freckles. Not the marks of beauty in our culture. In my insecurity, I overly concerned myself with what other people thought of me. Boldness? Not an ounce. But then Jesus got inside of me. And in time, as I came to know Him more intimately, I became bolder. Bold to speak of Him. Bold to speak to Him. Bold because of Him. He has slowly made me confident as He proved to me over and over who He is and who I am because of Christ. And He keeps on making me more confident. We don't make ourselves bold or confident. He makes us bold by the power of His Spirit.

In the Book of Acts we read, "Now when [the Jewish rulers and elders] saw the boldness of Peter and John, and perceived that they were uneducated, common men, they were astonished. And they recognized that they had been with Jesus" (Acts 4:13). Boldness in front of society's religious elite didn't come naturally to Peter and John. Bottom line, boldness marked them because they had been with Jesus. When we've been with Him—seen Him, experienced His presence—we can't help but boldly declare His glory. In the letter to the Ephesians, Paul reminds the church that in Christ we have boldness. His Spirit makes us bold. And in that boldness, we confidently declare Him and confidently approach the Holy of Holies because of who we are in Christ. *Amazing.*

Paul wrote this letter while imprisoned in Rome. And he asks the Ephesians not to lose heart over what he was suffering for them. To *lose heart* means to be weak. We lose heart when we look at our circumstances and then define God through the lens of what we see. For example, if things aren't going the way we want, we say, "Well God, things are really horrible in my life so You must not care. You must not love me. You must not see me."When we begin with circumstance, we lose heart. Because in that moment we forget who God is. Therefore, if we don't want to lose heart when suffering comes—because suffering will come as long as we live in this fallen world—it's vital that we remember a few purposes of suffering.

One, suffering gifts us with an opportunity to see the sufficiency of God. If I look back over my fortysomething years of living on this planet, I can absolutely see that my times of suffering—when by His grace I've turned to the Lord in the midst of the pain—became the sweetest seasons of experiencing the sufficiency of God. I wouldn't ask for suffering. I don't like walking through the fires of life. But in them God does indeed prove His sufficiency.

Two, suffering presents us with an opportunity to be comforted by God. No one knows the tiniest folds of our heart except the Lord. He alone knows every thought we think and every fear we quietly feed. He can comfort us like no other. The problem is we too quickly turn to things or people on this planet to find comfort. We overspend, overeat, overdrink, overcommit, and overshare—scrounging for a taste of soul comfort. Yet God Almighty stands ready and willing to comfort us more deeply and more fully than anyone or anything else ever could. Suffering presents us with fertile ground for experiencing divine comfort.

Three, suffering severs our sin's nerve endings. *What does that mean?* In my ESV Study Bible for 1 Peter 4:1–2, it is written in the notes that "when believers are willing to suffer, the nerve center of sin is severed in their lives. Although believers will never be totally free from sin in this life (see James 3:2; 1 John 1:8), when believers endure suffering for the sake of Christ they show that their purpose in life is not to live for their own pleasures but according to the will of God and for His glory." Suffering plays a significant role in killing sin's power over us. It presents yet another opportunity to die to self—the epicenter of sin. And freedom from the power of sin is a gift of God, even when it's packaged in unwanted circumstances.

Don't lose heart. We're not running this alone. Suffering isn't purposeless. God hasn't forgotten and He's never late. Keep on, eyes set on Him.

back to you

In what relationship or situation do you need to remember that God has a plan and He's always on time?

How have you experienced the goodness of God in the face of suffering? If you haven't yet, then write out a prayer to the Lord, asking Him to remind you of His truths the next time you enter into a season of suffering.

Share a time when someone else's suffering (suffering well) has encouraged you to walk by faith in your own journey.

What one thing from today's study do you want to remember?

DAY FIVE

Ephesians 3:14–19

Today we'll look at the power and example of prayer as seen in Ephesians 3. Ask the Lord to speak to your heart as we go through this text, especially regarding your own journey with prayer.

Read Ephesians 3:14–19. Write these verses in your journal.

What does today's text reveal about God?

God the Father:

God the Son (Jesus Christ):

God the Holy Spirit:

What does today's text reveal about humankind?

God prompts:

Did you catch it? Paul finished the parenthetical that he began in verse two and went back to his original thought. "For this reason," because Jew and Gentile are being built together into a dwelling place of the Lord, Paul then prays. He bows his knees before the Father. He gets low and intercedes. Why? Paul knows the necessity and power of prayer.

It's a mysterious intertwining. I don't understand how the sovereignty of God holds hands with the prayers of man.

I don't understand how the all-knowing, ruling Father takes into account the utterances of His children. But I know there's a tension between the two we must hold.

Scripture clearly teaches that God sovereignly reigns. He's in complete control (Matthew 10:26–31). He moves the heart of kings as He wills (Proverbs 21:1). He opens the eyes of the spiritually blind (Matthew 16:16–17). He directs weather and war (Job 38). Yet, at the very same time, we're instructed to pray (1 Thessalonians 5:17). We're commanded to pray (Ephesians 6:18). Faithful followers of old, even the Lord Jesus Himself, exemplify a life of purposeful intercession (Matthew 14:23; 26:36, 39; Luke 5:16; John 17). I don't understand how the two—God's sovereignty and man's prayers—perfectly intertwine. But I know they do. So, we pray.

But for what do we pray? One great place to start is in Scripture. We can look at the examples in the Word and pray like God's people have prayed for centuries. We can pray like our Lord prayed. Too often our prayers miss the entire point of this life. We're here to glorify the Lord God Almighty. We're here to receive and reflect His mysterious, scandalous love. But our prayers too often stay small. So let's look at what Paul prayed for the Ephesians.

First, he prayed that "according to the riches of his glory he may grant you to be strengthened with power through his Spirit in your inner being, so that Christ may dwell in your hearts through faith" (Ephesians 3:16–17). That's a powerful prayer! These are first-century Christians who faced severe threats of persecution on their lives. And Paul's first prayer was for divine strength. He asked the Father, "from whom every family in heaven and on earth is named," to strengthen their inner being (v. 15). He asked the Father to empower the Ephesians—no matter the earthly struggle or suffering—so that they would have inward strength through the power of God's Spirit. These are the riches of God's glory—to be inwardly strong regardless of circumstance.

I'm (finally) reading *The Hiding Place* by Corrie ten Boom. And let me just command you. If you haven't read it, then get it. Today. Don't pass go and don't collect $200. Go straight to the library or bookstore and get a copy. If you want to be spurred on in your faith journey, her story will spur you on. Talk about inner strength in the face of unbelievable suffering, ten Boom and her family were taken to a Nazi concentration camp because of their work to shelter persecuted Jews. Then after years of torturous conditions, she miraculously survived. But not just survived. She inwardly thrived through the strengthening of the Spirit of God though outwardly she slowly wasted away. This is a prayer request we desperately need.

Paul not only prayed for inner strength through the Spirit. He also asked that the Ephesians would be overwhelmed and overcome with the immeasurable love of God. He said in essence, "Father, give them strength to comprehend the expanse of Your great love." This kind of knowing goes beyond mental knowledge. It's more than knowing in our minds what God says about His love. Paul desired for the Ephesians—and all believers—to know in their spirits and in the depths of their bones the love of God. That kind of knowing changes us. It changes how we walk through trials. It changes how we respond to hurts. It changes how we sift through suffering. It changes how we see the other broken people around us.

Yes, we can pray for Sally's cousin's neighbor's lost false tooth. We can pray for a parking spot at the grocery store or a good seat at a coffee shop. Sure. But if we want to pray in a way that shifts the cosmos and truly strengthens our fellow brothers and sisters to walk powerfully on this planet, we look to the examples given in Scripture. "Lord God Almighty, fill them with all of your fullness in Christ."

back to you

Why do you think we struggle with prayer?

Think of someone in your life who's struggling. Following Paul's example, write out a prayer for this person using verses 16–19.

What one thing from today's study do you want to remember?

DAY SIX

Ephesians 3:20–21

Our glory-hungry world will knock on our heart's door today. But ask God to overwhelm you with the glory that our God alone deserves as we meditate on these two familiar verses from Ephesians. Rock our little world, Lord God Almighty.

Read Ephesians 3:20–21. Write these verses in your journal.

What does today's text reveal about God?

God the Father:

God the Son (Jesus Christ):

God the Holy Spirit:

What does today's text reveal about humankind?

God prompts:

If we've been in the church for a while, we've heard these verses. We've probably read them on coffee mugs or canvas prints, "Now to him who is able to do far more abundantly than all that we ask or think, according to the power at work within us, to him be glory in the church and in Christ Jesus throughout all generations, forever and ever. Amen" (Ephesians 3:20–21). But like I've said before, familiarity can breed complacency. So let's go phrase by phrase and ask God to undo us with His great glory.

Paul closes His prayer, "to him who is able to do." Whatever it is—as long as it doesn't go against His holy character—our God is able to do it. We're talking about the God who formed galaxies with a spoken word. We're talking about the God who raises dead people out of the grave, who parted waters so people could walk on dry ground, who sent insects by the gazillions as a plague, and who knows how many hairs are on all our heads. This is the God who is able. Whatever *it* is, He's able to do it. Nothing hinders His power. *Nothing*. No cancer. No persecution. No king. No earthly knowledge. His power remains unencumbered.

What does He do? "Far more abundantly than all that we ask or think." Not just abundantly. This God of the universe is able to do far more abundantly. Exceedingly abundantly. Whatever we dare ask for, or even think about as a possible solution to any and all situations on this planet, this God we worship is able to do exceedingly more than *that*.

But Paul goes even further. God not only possesses and moves in power unimaginable. God does things on planet Earth through us mere humans "according to the power at work within us." His power is at work within us to carry out His mission. The power within us explodes through and by the movement of His Spirit.

Before Jesus was crucified, He told His followers, "I tell you the truth: it is to your advantage that I go away, for if I do not go away, the Helper will not come to you. But if I go, I will send him to you" (John 16:7). And then later, after His Resurrection and before His ascension, He told His disciples, "You will receive power when the Holy Spirit has come upon you, and you will be my witnesses in Jerusalem and in all Judea and Samaria, and to the end of the earth" (Acts 1:8). That word *power* is the same Greek word in both the Acts text above and our

Ephesians text: *dunamis*. It means "miraculous power." We receive miraculous power through the indwelling Spirit of God to walk out this life by faith, come what may. This power of God is at work within us to do more than we could ever ask or think. The question is, are we aligning ourselves with and experiencing His power?

Imagine you're a billionaire but you don't know it. That'd be horrible. Instead of living the lavish life, you work hard to make ends meet, week after week fretting about how the next bill will get paid. But then you get a call from a banker who tells you that actually you're a billionaire. You've inherited billions of dollars from a long lost uncle, and the money now quietly sits untouched. You have a choice. You could keep on living like a pauper, or you could tap into your inheritance and live the life of which you've always dreamed. Either way you're a billionaire. But if you don't tap into the power of the billions of dollars, you'll never experience the life it could give you.

The analogy falls short, but we've been given a powerful inheritance in Christ, both in the life to come but even now through the gift of His Spirit. Yet so many of us live as if we have no power to overcome the pressures of our earthly struggles. We live as though we're paupers rather than children of the King of kings.

The God of the universe is able to do *more* than we could even imagine in our most imaginative moment through us by the power of His Spirit. It's to Him that we give the glory. *Let that sink in for a minute.* He remains forever worthy of glory "in the church and in Christ Jesus throughout all generations, forever and ever. Amen" (Ephesians 3:21). Paul pretty much painted the strokes as broad and as wide as he could. God is to be glorified "throughout all generations, forever and ever.

Amen." There will never be a time, ever, from now until all eternity when He's not worthy to be praised.

That means even when we don't understand His allowances in our lives, He's worthy to be praised. Even when things painfully derail our plans, He's worthy to be praised. Even when our shortsighted vision tempts us toward an adult temper tantrum, He's worthy to be praised. To Him be all glory forever. Amen.

back to you

How do we as humans seek our own glory? Give examples.

What is one of your most continual prayers?

Now, personalize and write verse 20 as a reminder for the next time the prayer request you wrote above comes to mind. You may begin with something like, "God, I remind myself today that You are able . . ."

What one thing from today's study do you want to remember?

week four

Unifying Love

Ephesians 4

DAY ONE

Ephesians 4:1–6

We've made it about halfway through Paul's letter to the Ephesians. We've spent the last three weeks looking at how God's love came down to earth through Christ. Now we're going to switch gears and look at how He intends for His love to flow out of us into this world. And I must say . . . some of Paul's words will step all over our toes and leave them bruised. But if the Lord convicts, it's in love. He desires that we walk in the abundance Christ died to give. Pray that we may have ears to hear His voice.

Read Ephesians 4:1–6. Write these verses in your journal.

What does today's text reveal about God?

God the Father:

God the Son (Jesus Christ):

God the Holy Spirit:

What does today's text reveal about humankind?

God prompts:

Paul spent Ephesians 1—3 overwhelmed with the glory of God and the grace given to us through Christ. He detailed the gospel message and prayed fervently that the Ephesians would know _that they know_ the depth and height and width of God's love. Because only after we grasp the vast extent of God's love that came down through Christ—our souls being deeply rooted in His great love—are we equipped to pour out His love onto the world around us. The last three chapters of this letter look at that outpouring of His love onto the world through us as His children.

Paul begins Ephesians 4 with "I therefore." In other words, because of all he said about the love and mercy of God, he urges them (and us) to "walk in a manner worthy of the calling to which you have been called" (v. 1). Because of whom God is and who we are in Him, He beseeches us to walk out our earthly lives in a way that reflects Him.

I often tell my kids, "Remember whose you are and who you represent!" I sometimes say it with angst and urgency when I don't want them to act a fool in public. _Because, image._ But other times (when I'm more in tune with the Spirit) I say it as a reminder that because they have come by faith to Christ, they are children of God. I say it as a reminder that their identity as God's son or daughter has implications. There's no space for fear within our true identity as a child of God. There's no room for hate within our true identity. There's no allowance for selfishness within our true identity. There's no excuse for divisiveness within our true identity. They forget. I forget. We forget that our identity as blood-bought children of the Most High has profound implications upon how we interact in this world.

Paul starts this section by explaining that to walk worthy of the calling as children of God means we will "bear with one another in love" (v. 2). How we bear with one another reflects whether or not we've truly received and experienced the love of God in Christ through the indwelling Holy Spirit.

To bear means "(figuratively) put up with, to endure, forbear, suffer." *Ouch.* It's little trouble to bear with those who are easy to love. But let's be honest. Some people are hard to love. People hurt us, betray us, sin against us, ignore us, and confuse us. But, lest we forget, we do the same to others. We're all on a journey of being sanctified by the Spirit, and in the meantime our mess rubs up against other people's mess and relationships get messy. Yet to walk worthy of the call as children of God we're to endure and bear with other fallen people *in love*.

If that isn't challenging enough, here's the real kicker. Even if we, in our flesh, can *externally* bear with another, we can't transform our internal self to truly bear with another *in love*. True bearing in love is a work of God's Spirit within us. It's Him giving us eyes to see the heart behind the words and actions of others and the desire to spur them on to live in the freedom of Christ. We, in eagerness to "maintain the unity of the Spirit in the bond of peace" press into the Lord God through worship and prayer (v. 3). He does the work of gentleness, humility, and patience.

The word *eager* in verse three means "to use speed, to make effort, be diligent." That convicts me because there have been relationships in my life that prove difficult to bear in love, and instead of being eager and diligent to maintain unity in the Spirit, I've given up and moved on. However, enduring with one another in love shows that we're eager to maintain the unity of the Spirit. Unity of the Spirit is God's gift through Christ. Unity reflects Him. Our call as His children is to maintain, or keep, the unity.

Paul finishes this section with reminders of the oneness or unity found in God: "There is one body and one Spirit—just as you were called to the one hope that belongs to your call—one Lord, one faith, one baptism, one God and Father of all, who is over all and through all and in all" (vv. 4–6). He pretty much nails it down. In God, there is no place for disunity. God's call is to oneness. Oneness in Him and with Him and with His people.

Earthly relationships struggle. We can't make others dwell in unity with us. That's not even our job. Our call is to bear in love. Our call is to maintain unity, with eagerness, as much as depends upon us, remembering that our good God is over all and through all and in all. May we walk worthy of the call.

back to you

Think of someone in your life that you're called to bear with. Do you see marks of God's Spirit—gentleness, humility, and patience—as you endure in that relationship? Give an example.

If not, spend some time confessing to the Lord, and ask Him to work humility, gentleness, and patience in you toward that person. If so, praise Him for His faithful working.

How could you show eagerness to maintain unity today in one of your more difficult relationships?

What one thing from today's study do you want to remember?

DAY TWO
Ephesians 4:7–10

In your time of prayer, ask the Lord to grace you with understanding regarding today's text. And ask that the magnitude of Christ's coming down to planet Earth would overwhelm you afresh. *Speak, Lord, Your children are listening.*

Read Ephesians 4:7–10. Write these verses in your journal.

What does today's text reveal about God?

God the Father:

God the Son (Jesus Christ):

God the Holy Spirit:

What does today's text reveal about humankind?

God prompts:

I've mentioned before that I was a wimpy kid. I was little and freckle-faced and didn't have an aggressive bone in my body. The thought of speaking in front of large groups sent me into a panic. But God did something crazy in me. When I started walking with Him, I knew He was calling me to speak and write. I was going to "declare on the rooftops what He speaks in the closet," a phrase I wrote in my journal one day while at seminary. And over time, He has unfolded more and more of that calling in my life.

In verse 7 of today's text, Paul says, "grace was given to each one of us according to the measure of Christ's gift." That doesn't mean that some of us have more saving grace than others. All of us through faith in Christ receive the full amount of saving grace. In this text, Paul refers to the grace we're given to *minister* to one another—the body of Christ. He's referring to the gifts that God gives to us as individuals, by His Spirit, in order that we can serve one another in love as He directs. Just as God has called me to publicly speak and write the things He says, God has gifted and called you to serve His body uniquely and powerfully. We'll talk more about this tomorrow.

We then come to verse eight, which feels a bit confusing on the first read. Paul is actually quoting Psalm 68:18. He then goes on in verses 9–10 to explain his interpretation of that Psalms text. Let's break those verses down.

First, Christ descended. Paul explains that Christ could have only ascended if He first descended to the lower regions, the earth. When Christ came to this planet, He dramatically descended. In the letter to the Philippians Paul tells us that Christ Jesus, "who, though he was in the form of God, did not count equality with God a thing to be grasped, but emptied himself, by taking the form of a servant, being born in the likeness of men. And being found in human form, he humbled himself by becoming obedient to the point of death, even death on a cross" (Philippians 2:6–8). Jesus descended, *down down down,* ultimately to the grave. He—equal with God the Father in His divinity—emptied Himself of His glory and took on the form of a servant. He came to His created earth as a baby to grow up into a man who would die as a sacrifice for His people. But not only die; Jesus died on a grotesque, humiliating Cross out of love for His creation. Jesus descended to the depths.

No matter how far you think your life has descended into sin or seeming chaos, Christ's love and sacrifice goes further. There's nothing we can do or have done in sin that His merciful descending doesn't reach and cover and cleanse. That's what's so amazing about grace. Jesus descended low to lift you and me out of our deepest of pits. I'm ever thankful.

But let's take it a step further. What about God's merciful descending for our enemies? What about Christ's sacrifice for the redemption of those who've hurt us or betrayed us? That's where I can get hung up. We love the thought of God's descending sacrifice for us. We shout "hallelujah" and do some praise dancing. But we want justice for our enemies. We want them to pay and pay big! That's messed up. When we forget that Jesus descended to cover all sin—even the sin of others that has directly affected us—and we demand they pay, He calls us the unforgiving, ungrateful, wicked servant (see Matthew 18:23–35). *May we remember.*

Christ descended.

Second, He ascended. He went to that grave bearing the wrath of a holy God for the sins of man. But sin and death could not hold the Son of God. Out from the grip of death, He arose. The chains of sin couldn't keep Him down. Death itself couldn't hold Him. He was greater. He was stronger than our human rebellion. He ascended from darkness into light and "led a host of captives" out of that grave (Ephesians 4:8). Who are the captives of sin and death? Every last one of us. But in Christ we're pulled out of that grip of sin. The chains are loosed. Freedom rings loud.

And if that isn't enough, when Christ sets us free from our bondage to sin, He gifts us. He gifts us with His Spirit. His Spirit gifts us with specific callings for the benefit of one another. His Spirit uses us to minister to one another in order that we might be further prepared for the ultimate gift of eternal life with our Maker. What mercy.

Jesus descended to earth—bearing the wrath of a holy God for the sins of man. And then He ascended through His Resurrection—defeating the consequences of that sin—leading us to freedom. In His victory, He gifts His people. He gifts His people to minister to one another. He gifts us that we might spur one another on to look more and more like our Lord and Savior Jesus Christ.

back to you

Have you ever struggled with shame over a certain sin? If shame could talk, what would it say to us about our sin?

Considering how far Jesus descended to redeem us, what would Jesus, in all His authority, say to shame?

What one thing from today's study do you want to remember?

DAY THREE
Ephesians 4:11–16

Before we continue our walk through Paul's words today, spend a few minutes in prayer asking the Lord to speak intimately and personally to you. Allow the fears and worries of life to rise to the surface of your mind, and then purposefully lay those things before Him, trusting that He is being faithful.

Read Ephesians 4:11–16. Write these verses in your journal.

What does today's text reveal about God?

God the Father:

God the Son (Jesus Christ):

God the Holy Spirit:

What does today's text reveal about humankind?

God prompts:

My journey as a blogger and then author has included some embarrassing covetousness along the way. For years I had twelve—count them, twelve—blog subscribers. My mom and my sister and ten other people who probably thought, *Bless her sweet heart. I'll subscribe.* I would write an 800-word blog post as one long paragraph without including a single image to keep the reader's attention. I would jealously stalk other bloggers and authors who seemed to have it all figured out. And I would secretly covet their journey while thinking, *God must be holding out on me.* That is, until God graciously, painfully, beautifully convicted me. He revealed that at the root of coveting another's journey and another's gifts lies a deep-seeded insecurity in who He has created me to be. *Blah. Insecurity stinks.* He then spent a lot of time doing more freedom work in me. *Praise.*

When we spend our time staring at the journey of another with longing eyes, we miss out on the joy and confidence in our own journey that God has for us to experience. And that is devastating. Because life is way too short to waste minutes and days doing or longing for someone else's job on planet Earth.

Bottom line, I need you. I need you to live out of the gifts God has given you. And you need me to live out of the gifts God has given me. We need one another. Paul refers to this interwoven relationship in the Body of Christ in today's text. He says that Christ has given apostles, prophets, evangelists, shepherds, and teachers to minister in the body. (And this is only a partial list of gifts in the Spirit!) Jesus, by the Holy Spirit, gifts us individually and purposefully for the good of the whole. Our callings will be distinctive. Our tasks will be unlike the person's beside us. But we need one another "for building up the body of Christ . . . to mature manhood" (Ephesians 4:12–13). In other words, Jesus gifts humans so that we would live out of our gifts, which equip and edify those around us, unto maturity in the faith.

I have three kids. They aren't mature. Sometimes I want to loudly say to them with slight aggression, "You're acting like such a child!" But just as those words are about to roll off of my tongue, I remember. *Ohhhh yeahhhh, you are a child.* Children are "tossed to and fro . . . and carried about with every wind of doctrine, by human cunning, by craftiness in deceitful schemes" (v. 14).

I remember being an immature child carried away by deceitful schemes. One summer at my cousin's house, we went to the mailbox only to find out that my uncle "MAY HAVE WON A MILLION DOLLARS." With great joy and visions of grandeur, we presented that gold envelope over dinner as though it was the answer to all his earthly prayers. *Deceitful schemes.* Children tossed to and fro.

But we too can be children of the faith. We too, even if we've claimed Christ as Lord for years and years, could still be a child at heart—tossed to and fro by the things of this world. Children in the faith stand on circumstance instead of the promises of Christ. Children allow the trials of life to crush their hope. Children allow fear to steal their peace. Children of the faith in grown-up bodies bounce around all over the place instead of standing firm on the Rock. Christ gifts humans with abilities in the Spirit to speak and minister to one another so that we would all grow up to maturity in the faith, "to the measure of the stature of the fullness of Christ" (v. 13). That's a tall order!

If we've named Christ as Lord and are sealed with His Spirit, then we're being conformed into the image of Christ. The image of Jesus Christ! We've *been* conformed in that we're sons and daughters through adoption. And we're *being* conformed through the sanctification of His Spirit. And His plan includes our brothers and sisters speaking the truths of God with love into our lives, so that we all "grow up in every way into Him who is the head, into Christ" (v. 15). When we're all doing our part—living out of our individual gifts, speaking the truth in love to our neighbor—individuals grow up, and the body as a whole grows up, in love.

Our good God, through the working of His Spirit in and through us, is making us mature in Christ. His love came down and then graciously comes out of us for the benefit of the whole.

back to you

How has God gifted you to minister to other believers? If you haven't thought much about it until now, take some time to pray and seek wise counsel from someone older in the faith. If we name Christ as Lord, then His Spirit gifts each of us.

Share a time when someone helped to build you up in the faith.

What one thing from today's study do you want to remember?

DAY FOUR

Ephesians 4:17–24

May the Lord graciously speak to us today. Spend a couple of minutes in prayer and then open His Word expecting to meet with Him.

Read Ephesians 4:17–24. Write these verses in your journal.

What does today's text reveal about God?

God the Father:

God the Son (Jesus Christ):

God the Holy Spirit:

What does today's text reveal about humankind?

_____ God prompts:

I have a love/hate relationship with big superstores. I love that I can pick up shampoo and a rotisserie chicken and some fresh flowers and a new TV, at competitive prices, all with one stop. But something happens to humans when we step into the doors of a mega discount store. I don't have any scientific proof, but it would appear that there exists an invisible force field that sucks out people's brains when we step through those sliding doors. Take, for example, the cart stealer.

One afternoon, I spent (what felt like) hours or maybe months walking around the store gathering all the things. I parked my cart on the stationery aisle, walked to the next aisle—the nail polish aisle—spent less than two minutes searching for that last item on my list, only to come *back* to the stationery aisle to find my cart gone and all of my items stuffed onto the shelves in front of me. All of my items stuffed onto the shelves. With the cart stolen. Seriously? Who does that? *People whose brains have been sucked out of their heads do that.*

How does this relate to Paul and the Ephesians? "You must no longer walk as the Gentiles do, in the futility of their minds. They are darkened in their understanding, alienated from the life of God because of the ignorance that is in them, due to their hardness of heart" (Ephesians 4:17–18). Sometimes it's tempting to look at the life choices people make and think, *What is wrong with them?* But people act like people. We should totally and completely expect to be betrayed and hurt as we do life on this planet. It shouldn't surprise us when someone takes our shopping cart and stuffs the contents on the shelf. But if we've come to faith in Christ, we have a different calling.

Paul beseeches us not to walk like the rest of the world. He tells us not to tread around in our homes, in the grocery stores, in our schools, or at our workplaces like those who don't know Jesus. We're to "put off" the old self and "put on the new self" (vv. 22–24). The imagery of Paul's word choice implies us sinking down into a garment. We're to shed our old self because it no longer has power over us in Christ. And we need to clothe ourselves with our true identity, remembering whose we are. We are adopted children of the King. We're sons and daughters of the Most High. Our citizenship is in heaven (Philippians 3:19–20). Therefore, we must no longer walk like the rest of the world in the "futility of their minds."

Futility of the mind.

The mind is a powerful thing. Even the world at large recognizes the power of the mind with its appeal to positive thinking. But all thinking, even all "positive" thinking, doesn't reflect or honor the Lord. Paul says people of the world—the unrepentant and unredeemed—walk around on this earth with futile thinking. They listen to their hearts and believe what they feel. They callously reject the love of Christ and greedily practice all kinds of sin. But that's not who we are in Christ.

In Christ, we're "to be renewed in the spirit of [our] minds" (Ephesians 4:23). We've inherited the mind of Christ (Philippians 2:5). By God's Spirit, we no longer have to walk out our days like the rest of the world in our thinking—futile, darkened, ignorant, and calloused. We can learn to think on what's true, from one thought to the next, which will result in *acting* on what's true. Because every action follows a thought. It's how God made humans. We think and then we do.

My middle son—bless his sweet heart—doesn't have much natural space between his thoughts and his actions. *This will serve him well if God leads him into a career as a secret agent or soldier or jouster.* He'll do well with a job where quick, slightly impulsive decisions need to be made. But in everyday living as a schoolboy, while his flesh still has much say into his thought life, that small space between thought and action can get him into a bit of trouble. But I'm the same way when left to me. Even at forty-*ahem*-something, I still sometimes speak or do before filtering my thoughts through the lens of God's truth. But our Lord, rich in His mercy, continues to grow me and teach me the power of the pause. He continues to sanctify my mouth by sanctifying my heart and mind because what comes out of the mouth flows from the state of the heart.

In Ephesians, Paul says that they—those in the world—have "hardness of heart" (Ephesians 4:18). And we who have experienced the grace of Christ know the only solution to a hardened heart. A hard heart needs the Spirit of God to replace it with a heart of flesh. "And I will give you a new heart, and a new spirit I will put within you. And I will remove the heart of stone from your flesh and give you a heart of flesh. And I will put my Spirit within you, and cause you to walk in my statutes and be careful to obey my rules" (Ezekiel 36:26–27). God gives a new heart. God puts a new spirit within us. God removes the heart of stone. God gives the heart of flesh. God even causes us, by His Spirit, to walk in His ways.

We can't expect people who haven't experienced Jesus to walk like Jesus. We can't expect them to think like Jesus. We can't expect them to love us like Jesus loves us. But we—those who have submitted to and received the love of Christ—are not to walk out our minutes as if nothing has changed. God has replaced our heart of stone with a heart of flesh. His Spirit dwells within us. We won't do life perfectly. We'll continue to wrestle against our fleshly impulses. But from glory to glory, God stands ready to empower us to love like He loves, *even at the discount superstores.*

back to you

Share a time when you walked "as Gentiles do" and then God graciously convicted you.

How does your thought life impact your actions?

What would it look like to pause before doing or saying what you think? What could you do in that pause to filter your thoughts through the lens of truth?

What one thing from today's study do you want to remember?

Ephesians 4:25–29

We start getting into some of the nitty gritty of everyday living in today's text. So prepare yourself. Toes will be bruised. But God only reveals areas of weakness in order that He may restore and redeem. Pray that He graciously ministers to us as we read.

Read Ephesians 4:25–29. Write these verses in your journal.

What does today's text reveal about God?

God the Father:

God the Son (Jesus Christ):

God the Holy Spirit:

What does today's text reveal about humankind?

God prompts:

All of you type-A people are going to be tempted to create a color-coded checklist from today's verses. *Do this. Don't do that.* And though lists have their good purposes in life, God calls us to more than do's and don'ts. God calls us to relationship. He calls us to dance with Him through the moments of our days. So I pray that these verses can serve as markers. I pray we let them reveal how we're living in the old self or putting on the new self. We all struggle at times. We're all in process. But the hope is that God, by His Spirit, will continue to grow and change us to look more and more like Jesus.

Verse 25 comes after Paul had beseeched the Ephesians (and us) not to walk through life as the Gentiles walk. He had just explained that we as Christ followers are to put off the old and put on the new. We're to step into the clothing that was purchased through Christ's blood for God's adopted children. Today's text contrasts these two opposing realities—the old versus the new.

First, Paul pointed out falsehood (aka lying). The old self lies. One of my children, who shall remain nameless, still reveals his submission to his old self nearly every time I ask if he has brushed his teeth. Oh, I know he hasn't. I can smell the rankness coming from his mouth all the way across the bedroom. *Falsehood.* But we mature adults don't lie about whether or not we've brushed our teeth. No, we're way more adept. We present falsehood so cunningly we don't even realize it's falsehood. When we act a certain way seeking to gain the approval of others (that we may not even like), that's falsehood. That's the old self. That's what Paul tells us to put off. Because in Christ—in the new self—we're free to be us! We're free to be in process. We're free to bless others with words of life because we're so secure in who God has made us to be. Falsehood doesn't belong in the new self.

Second, Paul touched on anger. When my kids first reached the age when they could tell me no and stomp around in opposition to my authority, I jokingly told a friend, "I never used to have an issue with anger until I had kids." But anger is an emotion. It's a revelation of what's going on inside of us. Given enough pressure, anger will come out of us all. So when we *feel* anger, we have to peel back the emotion and look at what's underneath it. We have to honestly ask ourselves, "Why am I angry?" Because more often than not, our human anger roots itself in a selfish desire to control the people and circumstances around us rather than a desire to see the righteousness of God prevail. *That'll preach.*

When Paul says, "Be angry," he's not commanding us to go around shouting because we're impassioned (Ephesians 4:26). Anger is simply a reality for our human hearts. But when we feel anger, we must be on guard. We must purposefully, diligently, and carefully look at the root of that anger. If we let anger drive us—rather than the Holy Spirit of the Lord—we're going to end up hurting lots of people. Or we'll end up in prison. *Maybe both.* That's why the Lord has so much to say to us about anger.

James tells us point blank, "be . . . slow to anger; for the anger of man does not produce the righteousness of God" (James 1:19–20). Our reactive, angry eruptions will not and cannot change human hearts. Be slow to anger.

> *A hot-tempered man stirs up strife, but he who is slow to anger quiets contention.*
>
> —PROVERBS 15:18

> *A fool gives full vent to his spirit, but a wise man quietly holds it back.*
>
> —29:11

> *A man of wrath stirs up strife, and one given to anger*
> *causes much transgression.*
>
> —29:22

Anger will come. We're human. It's an emotion. And though most human anger is rooted in self, some things *should* make us feel anger—abortion, racial injustice, apathy for the orphan, neglect of the widow, and everything else that God hates. But even when righteous, the passion of anger can lead us astray. So beware. Anger will come; but may we not take its hand and allow it to lead us into sin, giving an "opportunity to the devil" (Ephesians 4:27).

Third, Paul mentioned stealing. He instructed the Ephesians that the new self wants to labor in honest work. Why? "So that he may have something to share with anyone in need" (v. 28). We labor, yes to have food and clothing for our family, but also in order that we may be able to give to those in need. *Labor to give.*

Finally, Paul stepped all over their toes (and mine!) with the words, "Let no corrupting talk come out of your mouths, but only such as is good for building up, as fits the occasion, that it may give grace to those who hear" (v. 29). Y'all. This one convicts. He says no corrupt talk. That means none. Not one word. *Ever.* Corrupt communication does not fit in the new self. That kind of talk isn't a part of the redeemed life. God gives us words as a gift to build up, not as a hammer to tear down. Words that tear down come from thoughts that tear down. Words point back to the thought life. What we meditate upon will eventually come out of our mouths. May God continue to teach us how to take our thoughts captive to truth that we may give grace to those who hear our words.

Remember, Paul's words aren't meant to condemn. They're meant to inspire us to commune with our good God. They're meant to lead us into places of self-reflection, repentance, prayer, and then gratitude for His great grace.

<u>back to you</u>

How have you struggled with falsehood as a believer? One way to answer this is to think about how you are building your image on social media.

What do you do (or what could you do) when you feel the emotion of anger in order not to sin in your anger?

How have you seen the power of words in your own life? (Either for building up or tearing down.)

Write out verse 29 as a personal prayer to the Lord over your own use of words.

What one thing from today's study do you want to remember?

DAY SIX
Ephesians 4:30–32

Take a couple of minutes to allow your current fears or worries to rise to the surface of your mind. Then purposefully lay those concerns, one by one, before the Lord in prayer. Ask Him to speak to your heart by His Spirit as we glean from His Word today. Then trust that He will.

Read Ephesians 4:30–32. Write these verses in your journal.

What does today's text reveal about God?

God the Father:

God the Son (Jesus Christ):

God the Holy Spirit:

What does today's text reveal about humankind?

God prompts:

In the time of Moses, God's presence went with His people in a tent. Later, His people built a Tabernacle for the earthly manifestation of the presence of God. Next, Solomon built a glorious Temple for the abiding presence of God. Then Jesus Himself came to earth. Jesus was the temple of God—the earthly embodiment of His glory. Now, we who have received Jesus are the temple of God (1 Corinthians 3:16). You and me! That should totally and completely overwhelm us. We embody the presence of God here on planet Earth. His very Spirit lives inside us—the Almighty in earthly jars of clay. And we learn in today's text that we humans, when walking in our old self, can grieve Him (Ephesians 4:30).

To grieve means "to distress, to cause to be sad or be in heaviness, to make sorry." As the temple of God, our behavior (including our heart meditations) can cause the Spirit of God to be sad or heavy or distressed within us. You and I can grieve Him. And that grieves me. Because I know that I do that. I think about things, which eventually come out of my mouth, that grieve the Lord God. And those ways aren't marks of the new self.

My dear friend, Francie Winslow (for whom you should definitely search online and from whose wisdom you should definitely glean), has often said to me in our conversations about the Lord, "I want the Spirit of God to be at home in me." She desires for the Spirit of God to be welcomed and free to speak in her—not grieved and sorrowful. When we walk around in our old self, we grieve the Spirit of God. He has sealed us until the day of redemption. We're His. In God's mercy, He will never leave us or forsake us. We're permanently marked by Him. But we can grieve Him. And when we grieve Him, if we don't respond to His conviction, we may grow numb to His voice. Like a child with his fingers in his ears, in essence we say, "I'd rather listen to my old self rather than Your leading, God." And what a tragedy to ignore the voice of the Spirit of God Almighty.

Thankfully, in His mercy, God responds to the repentant. Because of Jesus, we're invited to repent when we grieve Him, and He promises to cleanse us from all unrighteousness (1 John 1:9). He mercifully gives us ears to hear His Spirit again and again because of the blood of Christ.

Paul finishes up the chapter with another comparison: old versus new. The old self lives in bitterness and wrath and anger and clamor and slander and malice. The old self keeps its proverbial eyes on the people of planet Earth, waiting to be offended by anyone and everyone that crosses it. The old self holds grudges and speaks poorly of others. It gossips in order to make itself look better. It seethes, sometimes behind a fake smile. It lashes out and stands on its supposed rights. It grieves the Holy Spirit of God.

But in Christ there's a new way. We can put on the new self. The Spirit of God marks the new self with kindness, tender-heartedness, and forgiveness, as God in Christ forgives us. This is one of those painful, hard aspects of the new self because it means true death to the self-life. As long as we live on this planet people will hurt us and we'll hurt them. It happens because we're all shortsighted and selfish by nature. We're all in process. The real challenge for us, in the new self, is to not grieve the Spirit of God with bitterness and deep-seeded anger. Rather, the call is to remember how Christ forgave us— fully, completely, and sacrificially. And likewise, we're called to forgive others the same way—fully, completely, and sacri-ficially. But let's look at forgiveness a bit because forgiveness can get murky when dealing with messy relationships.

Forgiveness means to release someone from the punishment we may think they deserve. It means we release them from our judgment and entrust them to the Lord as judge. We pardon. Jesus gives us the ultimate example of how to think about those who wrong us. When Jesus was reviled, "he did not revile in return; when he suffered, he did not threaten, but continued entrusting himself to him who judges justly" (1 Peter 2:23). When on a splintery Cross, bleeding for the sins of man, He looked at His accusers and said, "Father, forgive them, for they know not what they do" (Luke 23:34). Jesus found full rest in the Father's sovereign plan, even in the face of betrayers, because His earthly life and soul abundance wasn't tied to humans. Jesus found complete security in His oneness with the Father. Therefore, unforgiveness had no place in Him.

Forgiveness, however, is not the same as reconciliation. Sometimes we equate the two. We think that if we've truly forgiven, then the messy relationships of life wouldn't be so messy. But forgiveness is a choice of the will before the Father. It's a state of the heart. Reconciliation, on the other hand, takes two people. Reconciliation after an offense begins with forgiveness but takes time and effort to fully realize. It involves a rebuilding of trust, God-honoring boundaries, and an investment of intimacy. Jesus totally and completely forgave those who betrayed Him. He prayed for those who hurt Him. But forgiveness didn't always equate to reconciliation in His earthly relationships with those persons.

The new self will be marked with kindness, tenderheartedness, and forgiveness. When we see opposition to the new self in our minutes, may it simply serve as an invitation to repentance and dependence upon the Lord to renew and restore so His love may flow out of us.

back to you
_____

Thinking about your own tendencies or typical struggles with the old self, how do you feel that you most often grieve the Holy Spirit of God?

If you have a specific example of which you haven't repented, write out a prayer of confession and then thank Him that He cleanses.

Why do you think we struggle to forgive those who wrong us?

What one thing from today's study do you want to remember?

week five

Purifying Love

Ephesians 5

DAY ONE
Ephesians 5:1–5

Ask the Lord to grace you with a sweet time of conversation between you and Him as you open His Word. May His love continue to transform you.

Read Ephesians 5:1–5. Write these verses in your journal.

What does today's text reveal about God?

God the Father:

God the Son (Jesus Christ):

God the Holy Spirit:

What does today's text reveal about humankind?

God prompts:

My oldest child will celebrate her thirteenth birthday the year this book releases. *Lord, help me.* And now that her humor and sarcasm have appropriately developed, I realize: she imitates me. She literally sounds like me and does some of the same ridiculous things that I would do—like sing foolishly off-key as a wannabe opera singer to make her friends laugh. But I've noticed she also imitates my less-than-funny sides, like my control issues or desire for order. *Lord, help her.* The other day I heard her talking to her brothers, "Guys, you can't leave your stuff all over the kitchen island. The kitchen isn't a home for your things. Go put it away!" *Have mercy.* But here's the crazy part. She's not trying to imitate me. She isn't thinking in her preteen brain, *I want to be like my mama.* No, ma'am. She just *is* like me. Why? Well, she's like me because she's *my* daughter—she has my genes. But she's also like me because she knows me so well. We spend time together. We do life together. And for better and for worse, I've rubbed off on her.

Paul begins this next section of his letter with a short introduction. He tells us, as "beloved children" of God—adopted through the fragrant offering and sacrifice of Christ—that we should imitate the Lord (Ephesians 5:1). However, when Paul tells us to imitate God, he means more than an external copying. Just as my daughter doesn't have to *think* to be like me, as children of God, sealed with His Spirit, we have His genes, so to speak. We have the Father's spiritual DNA. And that spiritual reality *will* affect our external behavior.

But not only that. As children who spend time with our Father—listening to His voice, seeking His face, and loving His presence—through the transforming work of His Spirit, we *will* imitate Him more and more. It's the sanctification process. Yes, we have sin that tries to entangle us. Yes, sanctification takes a lifetime. Yes, we need to be mentally engaged in the war against the enemy and the flesh. But the Lord works *in* us to bring about an *internal* transformation evidenced by external manifestations of His ways. *Imitators of God.*

As we move forward in these practical portions of the Book of Ephesians, remember, we need to be on guard not to read these passages as a long list of do's and don'ts. It's vital that we read God's Word regarding external behavior as evidence of an internal reality. If we see that we're involved in sexual immorality, foolish talk, crude joking, and covetousness, as Paul mentions, may it serve as a means of conviction rather than condemnation. May it serve as an invitation to humble ourselves before a holy God, seeking His forgiveness, restoration, and strength to overcome.

Paul tells us in verse two, as imitators of God, we're to walk in love. The call upon Jesus followers remains so simple *in theory.* It's the point of this very book. It's the crux of Jesus' instructions to His followers: *Love.* Walk our days in love. Love God and love people. This will forever be the point of life.

> *You shall love the Lord your God with all your heart and with all your soul and with all your mind. This is the great and first commandment. And a second is like it: You shall love your neighbor as yourself. On these two commandments depend all the Law and the Prophets.*
>
> —MATTHEW 22:37–40

As Paul moves forward, he reveals what walking in love will and won't look like. As beloved children of God walking in love, "sexual immorality and all impurity or covetousness must not even be named among you" (Ephesians 5:3). *Not even named.* Paul is saying that these things don't belong in us anymore.

They don't fit within our identity as beloved children of the Holy God. They have the stench of the old self. "Let there be no filthiness nor foolish talk nor crude joking" (v. 4). These ways don't reflect our DNA in Christ. They don't reflect our glorious God. They're characteristics of the old. And if we live out of the old self, we forfeit the kingdom of God (v. 5).

We can fairly easily grasp the idea of God's heavenly kingdom. It makes sense that those who reject Jesus won't enter into the kingdom of God one day. They won't experience His eternal presence. But Jesus, and then Paul, refers to much more than a heavenly, one-day-in-the-future kingdom of God. When the Bible speaks of the kingdom of God, it means that even now, on planet Earth, humans with the indwelling Spirit of God can experience the kingdom of God. We get a taste of His loving, powerful reign. We get a taste of the freedom and joy and wholeness God intends for His creation.

Again, Paul's words are meant to reveal the state of our heart. If these things are named among us—if sexual immorality and covetousness and crude joking plague our hearts and days—then may it be an invitation to repentance. May it serve as sweet conviction that takes us to our knees in dependence upon our gracious Savior and His sweet smelling sacrifice. The Lord Jesus died so that we could live *kingdom* lives even on this planet.

---

back to you

Think of a time when you tried your hardest to imitate someone because you really wanted to be like them. How long did the imitation last?

Why does human effort to imitate not work?

How were you challenged or convicted today? How do you see the old self trying to rise up in your own life?

Write a prayer of repentance and thanksgiving.

What one thing from today's study do you want to remember?

DAY TWO

Ephesians 5:6–10

Today let's ask the Lord to shine His good, pure light on any darkness in our souls. Let's ask Him to expose anything taking up residence in us that doesn't reflect Him. He's so good to lead. He's so gracious to restore.

Read Ephesians 5:6–10. Write these verses in your journal.

What does today's text reveal about God?

God the Father:

God the Son (Jesus Christ):

God the Holy Spirit:

What does today's text reveal about humankind?

God prompts:

We like love. People generally accept the idea of God's love. We humans like to think happy thoughts about God's love for us. *Yay, Jesus loves me. He died for me. I'm forgiven! Grace!* We like that part of the story. We like that Jesus took the punishment we deserve. However, that's not the full picture. The full gospel declares Jesus' death and Resurrection while also demanding *our* death and resurrection. To follow Him, we must die to *ourselves* that He might raise us up to *new* life. *People don't like dying.* We humans would rather keep on living *our* lives, protecting *our* sin, because . . . well . . . we just like it. We like our sin. We like doing what *we* want to do. And in efforts to preach something a little more palatable, the cultural church at large has petted man's sin, in essence saying, "You don't have to die to your sin. Jesus forgives. Be you!"

Here's the problem. You—and I—are straight up wicked apart from Jesus. Our desires are twisted. Our hopes are selfish. Our agendas are tainted. Saying we can accept Jesus' love without a call to the crucifixion of self isn't the gospel. Yet, for centuries this false idea has been declared.

Paul addresses this heresy in Ephesians 5:6, "Let no one deceive you with empty words, for because of these things the wrath of God comes upon the sons of disobedience." I've said it before but I'm going to say it again. Words have power! Paul tells us that words can deceive us! Empty words. Vain words. Words without substance. Words that don't come from the heart of God have the power to lead us astray. That's sobering!

The empty, deceptive words Paul references in verse 6 are words that affirm "these things" in the life of someone who says they follow Jesus. What things? The things from verses 3–5—sexual immorality, covetousness, filthiness, foolish talk, and crude joking. If we say we've received the love of Jesus by faith, yet we don't live repentant lives when sin rears its ugly head, then most likely, we're not His. Our lives evidence our hearts. If our lives have a pattern of sin and unrepentance, then we're more likely still a son of disobedience. Those aren't words meant to condemn. They're truths meant to lead us into sweet repentance before the Lord. He stands ready and willing to restore us to Himself. He died to give us the power to overcome the temptations of our flesh, not perfectly but progressively. In Christ, we are not at the mercy of our sin desires; we've been set free from the power and reign of sin through Christ. Free to not sin.

Paul then transitions with a "therefore" when he says, "Therefore do not become partners with them [sons of disobedience]" (v. 7). I remember when the Lord awakened me to His love after years of rebellious running. I was going out one night with my old friends doing sinful, selfish things that we *used* to do. And I remember thinking, *This isn't who I am anymore.* I knew it. Not just mentally. I knew deep down where His Spirit had been stirred that I was a child of light. Partnering in sin with those who didn't know Him didn't fit me anymore. Partaking of the same sins of my old self didn't align with my identity as a daughter of the King.

Basically Paul told the Ephesians, "Don't partake in the same old sins with those who don't know Jesus. That's not who you are anymore." Remember, Paul isn't giving us a list of external don'ts. He's saying that if we're a child of the light then those old behaviors and old habits don't rule us anymore. Those things won't fit us anymore—like we've put on someone else's clothes. Instead of walking in those old things, he beckons us to tread all around this earthly life as "children of light" (v. 8).

How do we know if we're walking as children of light? Well, fruit will grow. Good, right, and true things will grow in our lives as fruit of walking in the light. Just as Paul describes in Galatians, love, joy, peace, patience, kindness, goodness, faithfulness, gentleness, and self-control will mark children of the light (Galatians 5:22–24). Over time, the Spirit of God, free and unhindered, grows these things in the life of the Jesus follower.

As we're imperfectly but steadily walking around this earth as children of light, Paul tells us to "try to discern what is pleasing to the Lord" (Ephesians 5:10). Yes, God gives us many clear directives in His Word. He tells us things to do and things not to do. He instructs us to forgive our enemies and speak only what builds others up. He guides us in the path of righteousness through the Proverbs. But life happens fast. Relationships with other humans often include complicated decisions. Paul tells us that as we walk around this earth we're to try to discern what would please the Lord.

This means that there will be times when we're not quite sure what to do. We won't exactly know how to be or where to go. But we try to discern what would please the Lord by staying in close communication with Him. God desires that we, His children, would walk our minutes in intimate communication with Him—seeking Him for direction, listening to His voice, following His prompts. To discern what would please Him means we stay close to Him. We talk with Him. We draw near to Him. And when we draw near we find that He's already there.

Walk as children of light because in Christ we are children of light.

back to you

_____

Did the Lord reveal any area of darkness in you through today's text? If so, write a prayer of repentance and then trust that God stands ready to empower you to overcome. (It may also be wise to seek out godly accountability as you aim to walk as a child of the light. We all sin. We all struggle. We need one another.)

How have you seen the power of words either deceive you or empower your walk with the Lord?

What does it look like in our everyday lives to discern what pleases the Lord? How do we stay in intimate communication with Him?

What one thing from today's study do you want to remember?

DAY THREE

Ephesians 5:11–17

It's gettin' real up in this letter to the Ephesians. Paul ain't messin' around. Let's pray we would be empowered to love the people around us well, especially when love means doing or saying hard things. Spend a couple of minutes asking God to prepare your heart for today's text before diving in.

Read Ephesians 5:11–17. Write these verses in your journal.

What does today's text reveal about God?

God the Father:

God the Son (Jesus Christ):

God the Holy Spirit:

What does today's text reveal about humankind?

God prompts: _____

For too long I lived deceived about the definition of *love*. I thought that love would stay quiet in the face of someone's sin, not confronting because that would be awkward and judgmental. I thought that love would pray and hope but not expose and address issues. I'm not sure why. It sounds ridiculously unloving when I type it out. But I don't like confrontation. I'd much prefer we all just get along or fake it until we do. That's my natural self. That's *still* my natural tendency I have to purposefully fight against. But that's not Jesus' way.

Out of God's great love for us, He exposes our sin. He exposes our sin, as His children, in order to heal us. He shines His light onto the darkness in us so that darkness will flee. And as His followers, we're called to the same. "Take no part in the unfruitful works of darkness, but instead expose them" (Ephesians 5:11). Refute them. Admonish them. In love, *as the Spirit of God leads*, we're called to humbly expose the sin of our fellow Christ followers. Not out of self-righteous pride or a belief we're any better *because we're not*. In fact, given the same circumstances, you and I would be tempted to do, and would probably *do*, the very same things we admonish in others. So we expose—not in harsh, condemning reprimands; rather, we lovingly expose the darkness in our fellow Christ followers because love desires freedom. Out of love we shine light so darkness won't prevail. *Not* exposing darkness is *not* loving.

You know what this means, don't you? If we're instructed to lovingly expose the sin in our fellow Christ followers, then our fellow Christ followers are instructed to lovingly expose *our* sin. *Ugh.* It's hard when *our* sin is exposed because we like ourselves. *A lot.* And even when we walk in sin, we defend our perspective and our actions. But here's a little phrase I've asked God to bury in my spirit so it will come out of my mouth when someone exposes my sin, "Thank you for telling me. I'll definitely pray about that." It's the very last thing I want to say when someone points out sin in me. What I *want* to do is give a long list of ways *they* could repent. But what if we just remember how messed up we are apart from Jesus and then stand ready to be helped in our journey of sanctification? What if we stood ready to hear rebuke—even if the person *doesn't* speak it lovingly? What if we actually meant it and then prayed for God's vision? *Lord, help us.*

Paul tells us to expose the darkness *in our fellow Christ followers.* Because of who we are in Christ, we're to walk in the light. *Walk in light!* That's why Paul inspires us to call our fellow Christ followers out of slumber—out of dark practices. Awake! Arise!

In his letter to the Romans, Paul uses similar terminology.

The night is far gone; the day is at hand. So then let us cast off the works of darkness and put on the armor of light. Let us walk properly as in the daytime, not in orgies and drunkenness, not in sexual immorality and sensuality, not in quarreling and jealousy. But put on the Lord Jesus Christ, and make no provision for the flesh, to gratify its desires.

—ROMANS 13:12–14

We as children of the light are to make "no provision for the flesh." The flesh will keep on demanding its own way. But may we make no provision for the darkness because this life is way too short. We don't have the luxury of time on planet Earth. We get one short chance to glorify God—to run our faith race with endurance.

I can definitely see the brevity of life when I look back on my years of mothering. It feels as though I blinked and my kids were half grown. Back when they were young—three kids under three years old—it seemed as though time went backwards in a maddening cycle of repetitive days. But now, by God's grace, I see. Our time on this planet goes by just as God describes. This life is a blink. A vapor. "You do not know what tomorrow will bring. What is your life? For you are a mist that appears for a little time and then vanishes" (James 4:14). If nothing else shakes us, then maybe a good dose of "your life is a mist" will awaken us. We have one chance at today—one chance at this season, this trial, this success, this failure. We have one chance to press into Jesus and reflect Him into this particular day. Paul instructs us to make the best use of the time "because the days are evil" (Ephesians 5:16).

It only takes a quick scan through the news channels to affirm the days are evil. Children are killing children. Adults are killing babies. Wars wage. Hate fills hearts. Skin color divides. Culture calls good evil and evil good. The days are wicked. *Severely* wicked. Yet, *yet*, greater is He in us than he that's in the world. "Little children, you are from God and have overcome them [those who do not confess Christ as Lord], for he who is in you is greater than he who is in the world" (1 John 4:4).

People rebel from the lordship of Christ. But the Spirit of God dwells within us as children of light. He wants to lead us in wisdom, not foolishness. Paul calls us to "understand what the will of the Lord is" (Ephesians 5:17). Understand that the call is to walk in light. Understand that it's God's will that we as His children walk our days in wisdom and in love. Arise. Awaken out of slumber that we would know the love of Christ. That love—true love—would flow out of us onto this broken world.

back to you

How would you define love based on today's text?

Share a time when God called you to love someone by lovingly exposing his or her sin. Or share a time when someone lovingly exposed your sin.

Is it easy or challenging for you to expose sin in others?

If you find that it's easy to expose others' sin, write a prayer asking God to soften your words and grace you with wisdom to know when to speak and when to stay silent. If you find it challenging, write a prayer asking God to give you boldness to speak loving exposure in the lives of fellow believers. May we love well.

What one thing from today's study do you want to remember?

DAY FOUR

Ephesians 5:18–21

Let's begin today by asking God to reveal our heart medita-tions. What's consuming your mind these days? What's taking up space in your soul? Lay those things, one by one, before Him in prayer. Then ask Him to grace you with perspective as we open His Word today.

Read Ephesians 5:18–21. Write these verses in your journal.

What does today's text reveal about God?

God the Father:

God the Son (Jesus Christ):

God the Holy Spirit:

What does today's text reveal about humankind?

God prompts:

OK, it's time for some Spirit talk. In the Book of Acts, when the Spirit of God fell upon the disciples at Pentecost, onlookers reacted in two primary ways. Some people praised God. Others ridiculed with the accusation, "They have *got* to be drunk."

Take a minute to read the account in Acts 2:1–21.

Why drunk? Because the Spirit caused them to say and do things that seemed crazy to those who weren't full of God's

Spirit. The Spirit caused them to speak "the mighty works of God" in languages that weren't their own (v. 11). It was unbelievable to some! *Literally.*

But that's what God's Spirit does. When we're full of His Spirit we have a boldness the world can't reconcile. We have inspiration and insight onlookers can't comprehend. Think about it. The very Spirit of God Himself—the eternal, all-knowing, all-powerful God—comes to live *inside* of us. As we read earlier, He comes to seal those who name Christ as Lord. He comes to dwell within us. *We* become His temple. But in today's text, Paul refers to something more than that original sealing of the Spirit. He refers to the *filling* of the Spirit.

In our Ephesians text, Paul says, "Do not get drunk with wine, for that is debauchery, but be filled with the Spirit" (5:18). Be filled. Or a clearer translation would be to keep on "being filled" with the Spirit. That word is present tense but in the passive voice. That means the filling is to happen this minute then the next, continually. *Present tense.* But the passive voice indicates we don't do it. We can't make ourselves filled. Our job is to fan the flame, so to speak, but God does the filling.

So how do we "fan the flame"? How do we keep on being filled? Paul gives us some insight. "Be filled with the Spirit, addressing one another in psalms and hymns and spiritual songs, singing and making melody to the Lord *with your heart*" (vv. 18–19, author's emphasis). With your heart. Throughout the Word of God, the Lord continually addresses the state of our hearts. It's one thing to *say* lovely things about God to another person. But it's another to *think* lovely things and *declare* praiseworthy things of the Lord *in our hearts*. To keep on being filled, we have to ask God to reveal the meditations of our hearts. Are songs of praise filling my soul? Or are thoughts of contempt and criticism and fear taking up space in me?

Whatever fills our hearts comes out of us. If praise fills our hearts, then praise will come out of our mouths, encouraging and lifting and loving those around us.

Paul continues, "Giving thanks always and for everything to God the Father in the name of our Lord Jesus Christ" (v. 20). Always and for everything. Always. And. For. Everything. Even the stuff we really don't like? Yep. Even the situations that make us want to scream and shout? Yep. Why? *How?* We can give thanks by remembering that God Almighty is forever good and remains in control. In love, He's sovereign. He can be trusted. When we're close to crumbling, through the questions and tears, we choose to give thanks always and for everything because our good God sits secure on the throne. We don't deny the earthly pain. We don't pretend as though everything is fine. We don't give thanks for the *struggle*. Rather, we preach truth to our souls *in the midst* of the struggle. He's *being* good, even when we can't see or comprehend. And more often than not, our Lord uses those hard things—the situations we want Him to change—as gifts to draw us more deeply into Himself.

We praise our God in our hearts. We give thanks to Him for everything, even the hard things.

And finally Paul instructs, "Submitting to one another out of reverence to Christ" (v. 21). We don't like the word *submit*. It rubs the all-American self-life completely the wrong way. But Paul doesn't say we submit because the other person is better or smarter or lovelier or . . . right-er. We submit, or yield, our self-will and our preferences out of reverence for Christ. We present our ideas but we don't demand our way. We share our insight but we don't pout when others disagree. In matters of preference, when sin isn't the issue, we yield to others *in reverence to Christ*.

Being filled with the Spirit throughout our days is a dance of intimacy with our God. We're filled as we choose to meditate on truth. We're filled as we walk in prayer—continually communing with the Father. We're filled as we repent of sin. We're filled as we praise the Lord with abandon—singing and dancing before Him. We're filled as we yield to others in reverence to our Lord. We *keep on being filled* as we press into Him moment by moment, come what may. And when we're filled with Him, we spill His love onto those our lives bump up against. *Love down and out.*

Yes, we're going to fail. We're going to be hormonal some days. *Thank you, estrogen.* We're going to holler at the driver who cuts us off. We're going to roll our eyes. We're going to keep on being human. But the glorious news is that we have the Spirit of God in us—the Spirit who raised Jesus from the grave—which means we're equipped to be *filled* with His Spirit. We're equipped to choose praise. We're equipped to choose submission. We're equipped to give thanks. We're equipped to wrestle against the enemy and the self-life and keep on being filled with the Spirit, reflecting our good God to a needy world.

back to you

None of us live life perfectly, but how would you describe the general state of your heart? Does praise of the Lord fill your heart? Or do you tend to meditate on fear/criticism/bitterness/etc.?

What most often triggers your flesh or old self to rise up?

What can you do (or what do you do) to keep on being filled with His Spirit today?

What one thing from today's study do you want to remember?

DAY FIVE

Ephesians 5:22–24

The next few days features practical instructions for wives, husbands, and children. Now, I know that some of you may be single and/or without children. However, God still has truths and promises waiting for you in these verses. So don't skip ahead. Pray and ask for God to open your eyes to things He may want you to know in this season of your life.

Also, know this: as we head into today's text, know that I mainly preached to myself as I prayed and typed. These are hard verses on the topic of submission. But obedience to God's call *forever* proves to be the way of blessing. So, before you dive in, ask the Lord to give you a heart that longs to obey Him as you glean from these short but powerful verses.

Read Ephesians 5:22–24. Write these verses in your journal.

What does today's text reveal about God?

    God the Father:

    God the Son (Jesus Christ):

    God the Holy Spirit:

What does today's text reveal about humankind?

God prompts: _____

Here's what's happening in the next portion of Paul's letter. He ended Ephesians 5:21 with, "submitting to one another out of reverence for Christ." Now, Paul details some earthly relationships in which we as Spirit-filled believers have the *privilege* of submitting. Yes, I typed that with slight sarcasm because, I know, it's not easy. Like I've said throughout the study, our self likes itself. It likes to do what it wants when it wants. It doesn't like someone to tell it what to do. It doesn't like someone to tell it how it's wrong. So the very heart of submission directly opposes the natural state of humans, which is one way God strips us of us. Today, we women get to hear Paul's exhortation to wives. A wife gets to submit to her earthly husband. Yes, *gets to*. It's an opportunity to die to self. Can I get an "amen"? *Pretty please?*

"Wives, submit to your own husbands, as to the Lord" (v. 22). Your *own* husband. First of all, Paul makes the distinction of marriage. He doesn't say, "Wives, you all submit to every man everywhere because you're women and they're men." He specifically refers to the marriage relationship. And the call to wives finds its basis in submission to the Lord. As wives submit, or yield, to the Lord, we're to also yield to our own husbands. Why? He tells us in verse 23, "For the husband is the head of the wife even as Christ is the head of the church, his body, and is himself its Savior." That's a mouthful of words. Let's break it down.

"The husband is the head of the wife." Wives willingly submit because of God's design for marriage. It's not that husbands are better. It's not that husbands are more spiritual. It's not that husbands are purer. It's not that husbands have a closer tie to the Lord. God designed men and women *both* as bearers of His image (Genesis 1:27). We are co-heirs of salvation. However, God designed men and women with different roles in the marriage relationship *to reflect Jesus to the world*. Ultimately, God designed marriage to be evangelistic. It's meant to be a picture to the world of Christ and the church. Our sin totally mars the picture God intends. Our selfishness taints it. Our expectations demand from it. But an evangelistic picture of marriage remains His plan. And in that vein, God designed men to be the head, or to symbolize the role of Christ, in the marriage relationship.

That means, when the world looks in at the way a godly husband leads his wife, they might say, "Wow, that husband loves his wife so beautifully and selflessly. He sacrifices on her behalf." That's what a head does. That's what Christ does for His own bride, the church. Likewise, when the world looks in at the way a godly wife responds to her husband, they might say, "Wow, she honors her husband so beautifully and selflessly. She follows his lead and respects him." That's the role of the body. That's how the church responds to Christ.

I know it gets complicated. *I know*—I'm married. And our marriage has been light-years away from "happily ever after." Sin has destroyed God's design for marriage. Wives demand their rights. Husbands insist upon their agenda. Self rises up.

And before I go any further, I want to clarify what submission *doesn't* mean. First, submission doesn't mean yielding to sin. If a husband is insisting that a wife follow him into sin, God does not call her to yield. Love means fighting for the good in another. Second, submission does not approve of abuse. In love, for the good of a soul or a home, tough boundaries will sometimes need to be prayerfully drawn. If you live in an abusive marriage, I encourage you to seek godly counsel and invite trusted believers into your journey. Abuse does not reflect the heart of God.

Those clarifications being made, our roles in marriage are meant to reflect Christ to the world. *Even if* one spouse doesn't live according to God's design, the other can still honor the Lord in his or her respective role. Even if a husband doesn't love his wife like Jesus, the wife can still reflect the Lord through her submission *as unto the Lord*. She can still choose, by the empowering of His Spirit, to yield to her husband as a reflection of the body of Christ.

Peter addresses this exact scenario in one of his letters, "Likewise, wives, be subject to your own husbands, so that even if some do not obey the word, they may be won without a word by that conduct of their wives, when they see your respectful and pure conduct" (1 Peter 3:1–2). "Likewise." You know who he's referencing? Jesus. Like Jesus who "was reviled, [but] he did not revile in return." Like Jesus who "when he suffered, he did not threaten" (2:23). Like Jesus, wives who find themselves in this particular situation, married to a husband who doesn't obey the Word, can reflect the Lord to the world. We continue "entrusting [ourselves] to him who judges justly" (v. 23). We reflect the Lord through His call upon *us* regardless of another. We yield to our husband, as unto the Lord, that maybe our husband might be won to Jesus through observing our respectful conduct. *A self-sacrificing call.*

The call upon wives, as a reflection of the gospel, is clear. Wives are to submit to their own husbands as unto the Lord. Granted there are some horrific marriages in supposed Christian homes where the most loving thing to do is to allow for difficult consequences to fall. However, God designed marriage to be evangelistic to a watching world. Wives have the opportunity to love the Lord by prayerfully, sacrificially, obeying His call to submission in the marriage relationship. May He strengthen us all for the call.

back to you

How have you viewed submission in the past? Positively or negatively, and why?

How does it encourage or challenge you to remember that marriage is ultimately designed for evangelism?

In light of the Scripture and truths we've talked about, how might you counsel a friend if you found out she was in an abusive marriage?

What one thing from today's study do you want to remember?

DAY SIX
Ephesians 5:25–33

Ask the Lord to open your eyes to His love in fresh ways today. Ask Him to speak to you regarding whatever situation weighs you down. After you've taken a couple of minutes to quiet yourself before Him, open to today's text.

Read Ephesians 5:25–33. Write these verses in your journal.

What does today's text reveal about God?

God the Father:

God the Son (Jesus Christ):

God the Holy Spirit:

What does today's text reveal about humankind?

God prompts:

I once heard a pastor say some powerful words to wives when he got to this particular text in his sermon. He said, "Wives, get back into *your* verses!" With all the books and conferences and workshops for "how to have a good Christian marriage," we women (I'm talking to myself too) have to take a step back and heed the word of caution. We can too quickly try to step into the Holy Spirit's role. We can too quickly write out verses on notecards for our beloved husband and slip them onto the dashboard of his car in an effort to kindly point out the ways he's not living up to God's plan for our marriage. We lock our eyes on our husband's behavior and how he isn't meeting our supposed needs. Then we bulldoze him with criticisms and creative ideas on how he can be more like Jesus. So I echo to you and to myself, "Wives, get back into *your* verses!"

But alas, this is a Bible study. So we're going to look more closely at what God says to husbands. But you have to promise me something. Promise me that later today you won't quote these verses to your husband, in Jesus' name, in an effort to change him. Only the Lord can change a heart.

OK, I think we're ready to move forward. Paul spends nearly three times the number of words talking to husbands about their role in the marriage as he does talking to wives. *Three times.* Seriously, the Lord sees the role of a husband as monumental. Yesterday, we saw that one purpose for marriage is to reflect Christ and the church to the world. The wife reflects the bride, the church. But the husband is called to reflect *Jesus* to the world through the marriage relationship. God tells him to love his wife "as Christ loved the church and gave himself up for her" (Ephesians 5:25). That's a big call. He instructs husbands to sacrificially and tenderly love their own wives. He tells husbands to lay down their lives for their wives. Husbands are to nourish and cherish their wives as Christ nourishes and cherishes *His* bride.

In God's description of a husband, there's no place for male domination or tyranny. There's no allowance for abusive talk or demanding hands. God's instructions to the husband create an environment in which the wife can joyfully serve the Lord as she reflects the bride of Christ in her marriage, encouraged by the sacrificial love of her spouse.

Ahhh. The birds chirp. The music plays. The rainbow glistens. This description of the husband's love is beautiful. It's poetic. It's . . . not always our experience on planet Earth. But again, these aren't our verses. Whether or not our husbands obey the Lord in their call is between them and God. We do not have the power to change a human heart. We're simply called to love and worship and reflect our God in whatever situations He takes us through. *He's* the One who changes hearts.

So let's shift a little and look at what these verses say about our Lord. Our Savior. Because even though God designed the husband to represent Christ in the marriage relationship, the husband does not *save* his wife. He doesn't wash his wife of her sin. Jesus redeems and sanctifies. "Husbands, love your wives, *as* Christ loved the church and gave himself up for her, that he might sanctify her, having cleansed her by the washing of water with the word, so that He might present the church to himself in splendor, without spot or wrinkle or any such thing, that she might be holy and without blemish" (vv. 25–27, author's emphasis).

It's crazy to me how much Jesus does through our salvation. I mean, He does everything. *He* gives *Himself* up for us. That *He* might sanctify us, making us holy. And *He* cleanses us "by the washing of water with the word," that *He* might present us to *Himself* in splendor.

Backspace. Backspace. Backspace. "Washing of water with the word"? What in the world does that mean? Well, it's powerful. Back in the beginning, God *spoke* the worlds into existence (see Genesis 1). He didn't think the worlds into existence. He didn't dance the worlds into existence. He *spoke* the worlds into existence. And throughout Scripture we see the power of the word of God.

We learn in the Book of John that Jesus *is* the Word of God. "In the beginning was the Word, and the Word was with God, and the Word was God" (John 1:1).

Let's break this verse down a bit. In the beginning was the Word of God—the truth of God. And that truth was God. Then the glorious part, "And the Word became flesh and dwelt among us, and we have seen his glory, glory as of the only Son from the Father, full of grace and truth" (v. 14). So the truth of God took on the form of human flesh in the person of Jesus. The Word—the Truth—became flesh. And the Word—Jesus— spoke human words to express divine truths. His words *are* truth, "The words that I [Jesus] have spoken to you *are* spirit and life" (John 6:63, author's emphasis).

OK, back to our Ephesians text. Jesus, our ultimate husband, washes us with water by the word. His words cleanse us. His truths breathe life in us. Which is why—*here's where we sound a little churchy*—we have to be in His Word. We literally— not figuratively—need the Word of God. We need to meditate on what He says. We need to preach His truths to our souls. We need to think on His Words. *Need*. Because in His mercy, He humbled Himself to speak human words—a sign of His sweet pursuit of us—that we might know Him. His Word washes us clean.

That makes me want to shout a little.

Love came down to earth in human form speaking divine truths with human words. May His love flow out of us unhindered.

back to you

When we read "someone else's verses" a good first step is to pray for that person who comes to mind. So write a prayer for your husband (or future husband) based upon today's text. You could begin something like this:

> Father, for the sake of Your glory and Your reflection through my marriage, I ask that you teach my husband...

Share a time when God used His Word to wash your soul. It could be that God encouraged you or convicted you through His Word.

How do you (or how could you) purposefully practice thinking on God's Word throughout your days?

What one thing from today's study do you want to remember?

week six

Empowering Love

Ephesians 6

DAY ONE
Ephesians 6:1–4

We've reached the last chapter of Ephesians! Which means that as I write, I'm both invigorated to see the finish line while also saddened to think our time together draws to a close. *A single tear slowly rolls down my cheek.* But we press on. And today's text again addresses specific relationships, namely that of children and parents. But even if that doesn't describe your current life stage, ask God to speak to you. His Word doesn't return void (see Isaiah 55:11). He has something for each of us in our time with Him today.

Read Ephesians 6:1–4. Write these verses in your journal.

What does today's text reveal about God?

God the Father:

God the Son (Jesus Christ):

God the Holy Spirit:

What does today's text reveal about humankind?

God prompts:

_____

I proved to be a quiet terror to my mom and dad in my teen years. I've mentioned it before, but I grew up as the preacher's kid. And I loved Jesus and loved my role in the church . . . until I started resenting it. Once the internal pressure to be "good" simmered beneath the surface of my life, I became a quiet terror. I could still play the role of the outwardly obedient child within the church building. But by high school, my heart and my friends ran far from Jesus and His ways. I did *not* obey my parents. I didn't *want* to obey my parents. I resented the *whole idea* of obeying my parents. But that's the heart of humankind when left to itself. We rebel against submission.

Paul addresses the submission of children in today's text, specifically the call upon children to obey their parents. In the text, Paul specifically instructs those under direct authority of a parent to obey. But if we're outside of our parents' house and authority, or even if we don't have earthly parents, the call to obey our heavenly Father remains.

When Paul says *obey* he means "to listen attentively; to heed or conform to a command or authority." But Paul doesn't mean simple *outward* obedience. There were plenty of times that I obeyed my parents *externally* while *internally* cursing their existence, wishing I lived in Mexico far *away* from them. That's not the obedience God looks for. He desires for us to have a heart that *willingly* obeys, that *wants* to obey, that stands ready to obey *as unto the Lord,* trusting that His instructions are for our good. For children, still under the leading of a parental figure, God calls to a *heart-level* obedience to parents. And if that convicts you, be encouraged. It convicts me as a child of God. We're all needy for the Lord's work in our hearts. He so graciously meets us right where we are. So, today you may need to humbly begin by asking God to grow your *desire* to obey from the heart. Then keep asking. He will faithfully answer.

However, just as a wife doesn't submit to a husband asking her to disobey the Lord, neither is a child instructed to follow a parent into disobedience. But those are tricky, complicated roads to navigate. So if that describes your situation, I would strongly suggest that you seek godly counsel as to how to respectfully address the issue. I pray you would seek the Lord's guidance as you walk that path. He's with you and promises to never leave or forsake you.

Now let's change perspectives and speak to my fellow parents—parents of physical children and parents of spiritual children in the faith. *Lord, help us all.* First, let's remember verses 1–3 aren't our verses in the parental role. Yes, we train up those coming behind us in the ways of the Lord, teaching them His Word and promises. But hollering at our children from across the house to "Obey your parents for this is right, Johnny!" isn't going to be very effective. That said, God commands us to teach our children that obedience brings blessing. And though that will mean reading the Word to those we're leading, the teaching of obedience will more effectively penetrate their soul as they see us living it out—us, individually and consistently, obeying the Lord, trusting that His ways are best even when we don't know exactly what He's up to.

We then get to Ephesians 6:4, "Fathers, do not provoke your children to anger, but bring them up in the discipline and instruction of the Lord." Paul specifically addresses fathers here, pointing again to the father's headship in the home. Fathers play a vital role in the development of a child. The lack of a father's godly leading has profound effects. But even in a home without the presence of a godly earthly father, hope remains. We have a Heavenly Father who moves and works in the hearts of children in spite of our earthly parental failures. He graciously stands in the gap. He miraculously answers prayers. He faithfully and sovereignly draws hearts to Himself. So, yes, the role of a father proves powerful. But women, let's not neglect to see our role as well.

Even though Paul addresses fathers, mothers too need to heed his warning. "Do not provoke your children to anger." Many (dare I say, most) children try hard to please their parents. They fail a lot, because they're human and they're children. They have a childlike perspective. But deep down, children desperately want to please their mom and dad. The danger for parents comes with our expectations.

I've come to a place in my parenting where I actually expect that my children will fail to obey me. Not because they *want* to disobey but simply because they're human, like me. *And I'm a mess apart from Jesus' intervention.* When I forget their flesh tendency, my response to their failure is tainted with shame and condemnation. When I *expect* obedience—usually out of the protection of my own image or fear of being out of control—I'm tempted to say in frustration, with a clinched jaw, "I expect you to obey me!" In essence, since you failed me, shame on you.

Not provoking to anger means we give people space to be in process. We walk with them through their struggles, teaching them the gracious words of their Maker. We stop depending on their obedience for *our* identity. *Oh, that's a word many of us need to meditate upon.* And we remember that parenthood is just as much a context for us to be transformed into the image of Christ as it is for them.

Love graciously came down through Christ. And as children or parents, love comes out in our interactions through these earthly relationships. *Lord, help us reflect You.*

back to you

Can you identify an area in your life where you are externally obeying while internally rebelling? Write a prayer of thanks to the Lord that He's merciful with our process, and then ask Him to grow a heart-level obedience.

How have you provoked others to anger? Try to tie your answer back to the idea of expectations.

What everyday practices can you put into place (if you haven't already) as you disciple others in the Lord?

What one thing from today's study do you want to remember?

Ephesians 6:5–9

It's so tempting to live life trying to please people when ultimately it's the pleasure of the Father that satisfies our souls. Start today with a time of prayer asking God to grow your desire to do His will from a sincere heart. Then open His Word ready to listen to what He has to say.

Read Ephesians 6:5–9. Write these verses in your journal.

What does today's text reveal about God?

God the Father:

God the Son (Jesus Christ):

God the Holy Spirit:

What does today's text reveal about humankind?

God prompts:

Before we get too far, I need to make one sweeping stroke of clarification regarding today's text. Paul isn't approving of or endorsing slavery. This letter isn't propaganda for or against the social constructs that existed in first-century Christendom. He's simply instructing *believing* bondservants and *believing* masters in how to live out those roles in a way that reflects the Lord.

According to the notes in my ESV Study Bible, when Paul wrote this letter, slaves, or bondservants, comprised approximately one-third of the population of Ephesus. This social structure typically included bondservants who were paying off a debt to a master rather than the forced, endless labor many of us may naturally assume because of North America's history. That said, bondservants of this day actually played a significant role in the family structure. Paul's address to bondservants would have been a natural progression after addressing the other familial roles within the home.

Even though we're not a bondservant within a physical, social structure, this text still applies to us. In fact, today's text touches on some deep truths that will step all over our toes in the most beautifully crushing sort of way.

First, Paul addresses the heart behind our submission in relationships. He says, "Obey . . . with a sincere heart, as you would Christ, not by the way of eye-service, as people-pleasers, but as bondservants of Christ, doing the will of God from the heart" (Ephesians 6:5–6). He tells us that it matters *why* we honor or obey or submit to those around us. If we do what someone asks with a smile on our face but contempt in our heart, it doesn't honor the Lord. If we get that thing our boss needs but curse him under our breath, it doesn't reflect Jesus. The Lord desires purity of *heart* in our submission to one another. And the only way to submit to others with a pure heart is if we live as a bondservant of Christ.

Live as a bondservant of Christ.

I know it's hard. Relationships are tough. People can be unreasonable and flat out mean at times. If humans aren't submitted to the lordship of Jesus, they live and move out of their own woundedness. And that can get very ugly. But Paul is telling us, in whatever relationships we find ourselves, to live as a bondservant of *Christ*. Keep our eyes on Jesus. Serve as though we're serving *Him*. Sure, people don't deserve it. But we didn't deserve the grace we received when Jesus brutally died for our sins. So when relationships are tough and seemingly unfair, we have to remember whom we serve. We serve our Lord.

Paul continues, saying we should serve as unto the Lord "knowing that whatever good anyone does, this he will receive back from the Lord, whether he is a bondservant or is free" (v. 8). I don't claim to know how things will go down when Jesus comes back to earth. And I don't hold to the version of the gospel that says God is like a genie in a bottle who gives material blessings to the faithful, usually in the form of cars and cashmere. However, there's no way around it. God honors those who glorify Him through their actions on this planet. God blesses those who, from a sincere heart, do good on this earth out of love for Him.

What will that look like? I have no definite idea. God's ways are not our ways. However, I *do* know whatever good anyone does, this he will receive back from the Lord. That's all I know. Honoring God through *sincere* good works will not be overlooked. God rewards His children.

Having my own children gives me a taste of this aspect of God's fatherly love. I adore rewarding my kids. I just do. But I don't love it when they *expect* me to reward them because they did something "good" for me to see. Like, "Look, Mom! I made my bed. Will you buy me some baseball cards?" What

I love is surprising them simply because I've seen them do a *sincere* good thing.

I recently took my kids to the park. It was just us hanging out until another mom arrived with her son. Her boy was about nine years old, and he had Down syndrome. My two wild young men were busy tackling/wrestling/too-aggressively-hurling one another in the sand volleyball court—*I was so proud*—when her son came over to observe. He watched my boys for a bit and then finally sat down in the sand. My sons caught his eye and stopped wrestling. Then my middle son went over and sat down with him. The boy's mom watched from a nearby bench, possibly waiting to see what my son would do, *possibly scarred from what other children have said or done.* My son just sat and eventually started playing with the boy. What did they play? They threw a water bottle lid back and forth. That's about when my heart crushed inside of me.

I sat on a swing watching and praying and utterly elated. My boy, by the absolute grace of Jesus, saw someone who had struggles different from his. From an imperfect but sincere heart, he engaged. And you know what I wanted to do? I wanted to buy him ice cream. I wanted to reward him. He wasn't expecting reward. He wasn't demanding reward. He simply did good and as his mama, I longed to reward him.

In a much more infinite, perfect way, God's like that. It pleases His father-heart when we imperfectly but sincerely do good to those around us. It pleases Him when we serve others with a good will as to the Lord. And He rewards.

Paul doesn't end there. He finishes this section with a word to masters. A word we can heed in any relationship in which we're the authority. "Stop your threatening" (v. 9). Stop taking advantage of the lead role we've been given. Instead, serve those under you as you would serve the Lord. That's humbling. But that's what Jesus did. He humbled Himself, taking on the form of a man and dying a humiliating death for you and me. He washed the dirty feet of His disciples. He served. A good leader selflessly serves while remembering that there's an ultimate Master who shows no partiality to human structures and earthly status.

Love came down and bowed low. Love calls us to do the same.

_____ back to you

Whom have you struggled to serve with a sincere heart?

Write a prayer of confession, and then ask the Lord to help you serve that person (those people) with sincerity of heart as if you're serving the Lord.

Think of a leadership role you currently hold. It may be at work or at church or in the home. How does it look to lead as Christ leads, without threatening?

What one thing from today's study do you want to remember?

DAY THREE

Ephesians 6:10–12

Today's verses give such needed perspective. But before diving in, spend a few minutes in prayer asking God to grace you with His perspective today, especially regarding those relationships or situations that cause you to struggle most. May His true Word invigorate your soul today.

Read Ephesians 6:10–12. Write these verses in your journal.

What does today's text reveal about God?

    God the Father:

    God the Son (Jesus Christ):

    God the Holy Spirit:

What does today's text reveal about humankind?

God prompts:

"Finally," Paul says, after all he has declared in his letter, "be strong *in the Lord* and in the strength of *his* might" (Ephesians 6:10, author's emphasis). True strength doesn't originate in us . . . or in a strong cup of coffee, *though I'm 100 percent in favor of a strong cup of coffee.* The strength we need to make it through this life on planet Earth can't be conjured up from our flesh. We're way too weak. The strength we need is *God's* strength. *His* strength carries us. *His* might empowers us. Be strong *in the Lord.* Those aren't just words to belt in song on a Sunday morning. *Though they are and we should.* Those are truths meant to turn our hearts to the Source of our strength that we might walk our days in victory, *especially on the days when we feel like we have zero strength left.*

But what does "be strong in the Lord" look like on Monday and Tuesday? What does it look like to be strong in the Lord when we feel as though we may crumble under the weight of our circumstances? It looks like communing with our Father. It looks like feasting on His Word. It looks like turning our hearts and minds to places of truth. "Fear not, for I am with you; be not dismayed, for I am your God; I will strengthen you, I will help you, I will uphold you with my righteous right hand" (Isaiah 41:10). That's *real* strength. His strength. And it's a promise.

On Monday and Tuesday and every other day we feast on His Word and His promises. But we weren't meant to do it alone. We also need to live authentically with other sisters in Christ so they can encourage us. We need others to speak words of courage into us. But they won't know we need a word of courage if we don't share our struggle.

Beneath all of the external choices we can make to be strong in the Lord, we have to remember that we're in the middle of a war. We need to keep wartime mentality.

I have two sons. And these two sons of mine have more energy than Chihuahuas hopped up on espresso. They're constantly grabbing and pushing and growling at one another. They're continually on the offense, aiming to pin the other to the ground with the force of a semi truck. *All in love, mostly.* So I picture my boys' gnarled up faces—feet ready to run and hands ready to engage—when I read today's verses. To them, life is a continual battle against an enemy, aka each other.

If we're going to experience the victory Jesus died to give, we *have* to remember that we are in the midst of a war. I'm not talking about a political war in a tangible land. No. I'm talking about the spiritual war that continually wages all around us. It's the war against the enemies of God in which they seek to steal, kill, and destroy our joy, peace, and hope (John 10:10). It *feels* as though a war wages against our husband or our in-laws or . . . the superstore clerk. It *feels* as though it's a war against the people we see with our physical eyes. But Paul clearly tells us that the war waging around us is "against the authorities, against the cosmic powers over this present darkness, against the spiritual forces of evil in the heavenly places" (Ephesians 6:12). The enemies of God continually speak lies to the children of God in efforts to steal our focus and drain our hope (John 8:44). And we fall prey day after day because we forget we're in the midst of a war.

So many lies plague us. I could write an entire book about the lies to which we give our heart's devotion. But for the sake of space and time, I'm going to only point out two (of the approximately 143) lies that I see us as God's children believing all too quickly. One, the lie that God isn't being good. And two, the lie that we are entitled to anything.

First, when we give heart space to the lie that God isn't being good, fear and worry become our companions. When we truly believe that God is being good, fear has to bow down. We may not know what God is doing. We may not understand His timing or allowances. But if we begin with the truth that God is indeed good to His children and that He's actively *being* good to His children, then there's no room for fear. Yes, it will be a wrestling to believe. Yes, we'll have to struggle against our wayward minds, taking our thoughts captive to truth over and over again. But what if we dared to believe that regardless of what we see, God is being good? We'd silence that lying enemy as we declare with boldness, "My God is being good, even in this!"

The second lie is entitlement. Minute by minute, the media feeds us the lie that we *deserve* this or that. We deserve that car. We deserve that dessert. We deserve that respect. We deserve that pair of boots we can't afford. We have a right . . . because we're us! And we're awesome! But that lie fuels two deadly situations. It fuels pride. And it fuels debt. Sip on this truth, sweet sister. The only thing we deserve is death. Remember, we were enemies of a holy God. We were children of wrath apart from Jesus' intervention. It's only because of the mercy of the Father that we don't get what we deserve. The money in our pocket is His. The breath in our lungs is His. In Christ, we're His. May we silence the enemy with praise of our gracious Lord who rescued us from what we truly deserve.

The enemy won't stop lying. Until Jesus comes again, he and his cohorts will continue to whisper lie after lie into our ears. But Paul tells us to "put on the whole armor of God, that you may be able to stand against the schemes of the devil" (Ephesians 6:11). Stand. Not fall prey. Stand. Not bow down to fear or hopelessness. It won't be easy. War never is. But it can be victorious. We *are* victorious in the strength *of the Lord.*

Press on, mighty warrior. Press on in Him.

back to you

When you feel physically or emotionally weak, what does it look like to "be strong in the Lord"?

Who (or what) do you feel like you're in a war against?

What lies are you prone to believe? Pray and look for the red flags of fear or worry to help identify the lies.

In light of the lie(s) you mentioned above, what truth(s) from God's Word do you want to remember when those lies tempt your heart's devotion? (Consider writing those truths on notecards and putting them on your bathroom mirror.)

What one thing from today's study do you want to remember?

DAY FOUR

Ephesians 6:13–18*a*

We're nearing the end of the letter to the Ephesians. But today's text is a vital portion of Paul's letter. Ask the Lord to grace you with further perspective and a new vigilance against the enemy today.

Read Ephesians 6:13–18a. Write these verses in your journal.

What does today's text reveal about God?

God the Father:

God the Son (Jesus Christ):

God the Holy Spirit:

What does today's text reveal about humankind?

God prompts:

Therefore. Because we're in a spiritual war against spiritual enemies, *therefore*, "take up the whole armor of God, that you may
be able to withstand in the evil day, and having done all, to
stand firm" (Ephesians 6:13). God's armor is *the only thing* that
will equip us against the enemy. We can't fight spiritual forces
with *physical* weapons. "For though we walk in the flesh, we are
not waging war according to the flesh. For the weapons of our
warfare are not of the flesh but have divine power to destroy
strongholds" (2 Corinthians 10:3–4). There's a spiritual war waging, and we need to wield spiritual weapons.

Paul tells us to stand. Don't sit down in defeat. Don't run
away. Don't lie down in fear. Stand up, child of God, and stand
firm, "having fastened on the belt of truth, and having put on
the breastplate of righteousness, and, as shoes for your feet,
having put on the readiness given by the gospel of peace"
(Ephesians 6:14–15).

The first three aspects of God's armor point to our identity
in Christ. These things must be secure *before* we stand against
the enemy. Otherwise defeat is sure.

The *belt of truth* must be fastened. That means we've
submitted to the truth of God, the truth of the gospel. We've
given ourselves over to Christ. We also need the *breastplate of
righteousness* upon our chest. Before a holy God, we humans
can't be righteous on our own. But through faith in Christ,
He imparts *his* righteousness to us. We can only stand firm
against the enemy if we're His—righteous because of faith
in Christ. Lastly, when the gospel has changed us and given
us a new identity, we naturally spread the *gospel of peace* to
those around us. *Tasting* the gospel of peace causes us to *speak*
about the gospel of peace. Like Peter and John declared: we
can't help but speak of Jesus (see Acts 4:20). Ultimately, these

three initial pieces of armor reflect our new identity—our genuine faith in the saving power of Christ.

Having these three pieces of our armor secure—in other words, our identity secure in Christ—Paul then addresses what to *do* in our circumstances. He tells us to take up the shield, "with which you can extinguish all the flaming darts of the evil one" (v. 16). Remember, the enemy comes at us with lies. And those lies sting. To fend off the enemy's fiery darts, we have to lift up the shield of faith. That means we need to learn how to preach truth to ourselves and to the enemy. We declare our faith in the character and promises of God when the enemy comes with a vengeance. Take up the shield of faith.

Along with the shield Paul tells us to take the helmet of salvation. The helmet guards the head. And do you know what's in that cute little head of yours? Your mind. *Lord, help us with our minds.* In 2.4 seconds my mind can take me to places I would be tempted to deny if publicly asked. It never ceases to amaze me how depraved my mind can be if I let it wander as it wills. We have to take our minds, our thoughts, captive to truth. If we don't, we will entertain some wicked things. Take up the helmet of salvation. By the power of the Spirit, we take our thoughts by the proverbial hand and lead them where we want them to go. We lead our minds into places of truth. *Because things get ugly when we don't.*

Next we take up "the sword of the Spirit, which is the word of God" (v. 17). I can't say this enough. We. Have. To. Know. The. Word. When the enemy came against Jesus with lies in the wilderness, Jesus declared to one lie after the other, "It is written" (see Matthew 4). We have to know what is written in order to fight off the lies of the enemy. Because you know what's scary? The enemy also quotes Scripture, but he quotes it out of context. If we aren't marinating in the Word of God, thinking on the Word of God, memorizing the Word of God, the enemy's lies will taste good to our self-egos. The enemy's lies will affirm our feelings and appeal to our vulnerabilities. Lift the sword, mighty warrior. Lift the sword of the Spirit and fight the lies of the enemy.

Lastly, but dare I say most importantly, behind and during and around every battle we fight on this planet, we're called to be "praying at all times in the Spirit, with all prayer and supplication" (Ephesians 6:18). At all times! God convicted me of this recently.

One of the lies I've believed over the years, *though I would have denied it*, is the lie that I can change someone else. The lie that God needs *my* help to change another person's heart. In my head I *knew* I couldn't change another person. But my actions revealed that I didn't actually *believe* it. For years and years I tried so hard to do things and say things and manipulate things in a way that would change another person until God spoke a word of sweet conviction. He said to my spirit one morning after time in His Word, "Lara, be vigilant in this battle." I talked back to my God, "I have, Lord! I've been vigilant! I've done so much! What else can I do?" And then with the very next beat of my heart I heard Him whisper to my soul, "Be vigilant in prayer."

This is another one of those topics to which entire books have been devoted. So I can't do the topic of prayer justice in this short space. But for our purposes let me shout in the most loving way to you, and to myself, "*Pray!* Pray at all times with all prayer." Our God is the defender. Our God is the healer. Our God is the builder. Our God is the One who stands ready to fight on our behalf if we'll just get out of the way and stand firm in Him.

With armor secure and raised high, may we pray continually to the One who has already won the war. May we stand firm
in His great love and fight the enemy with His armor secure.

_____ back to you

*In which relationship or circumstance do you think you're most
vulnerable to the enemy's fiery darts? Recognizing our vulnerabilities helps us stay on guard to the enemy's lies.*

*How would you describe your prayer life? What step could you
take today to bring prayer to an even more prominent place in
your life?*

*In light of today's text, write out a prayer in which you put on the
armor of God.*

What one thing from today's study do you want to remember?

_____ DAY FIVE
Ephesians 6:18b–20

Until Jesus comes back, a spiritual war will continue. Ask the
Lord to grace you with alertness today in the midst of the

battles. May the enemy not gain any ground in our souls and the souls of those we love today.

Read Ephesians 6:18b–20. Write these verses in your journal.

What does today's text reveal about God?

    God the Father:

    God the Son (Jesus Christ):

    God the Holy Spirit:

What does today's text reveal about humankind?

God prompts: _____

We all need others to hold us up through prayer because life's journey can be excruciating at times. Some days it feels like the enemy has us in his grip and Jesus is nowhere to be found. It *feels* as though we've been forgotten or discarded. But when we start thinking those thoughts of abandonment and fear, that's exactly the moment we need to remember what's true about our God and about the enemy. That's exactly when the prayers of others can hold us up.

In the Book of Job, we learn some important aspects about the enemy. Right out of the gate, Job is described as "blameless and upright, one who feared God and turned away from evil" (Job 1:1). Job loved God. He honored God. And he had much in regard to earthly blessings: children, land, livestock, and health. But then we get a glimpse behind the curtains of heaven at a conversation between God and Satan, in which the Lord God offers Job to Satan to be sifted. God offers Job to Satan *within the boundaries set by the Almighty.*

The enemy proceeds to strip Job of everything: his children, his earthly possessions, and his health. It was an excruciating season of severe suffering. And for the first 37 chapters of the book, the Lord remains silent as Job tries to process the depths of his travesty.

But we learn a key aspect about the enemy through the story of Job's suffering. The enemy can only go as far as God sovereignly allows. In the lives of God's children, the enemy can only do what God allows him to do for our *ultimate* good and God's *ultimate* glory. We can't possibly understand all God's ways. We can't possibly figure out all the *whys* behind every instance of suffering. But we can begin with truth. We can filter every attack of the enemy through the lens of God's character. We can believe that what the enemy means for evil, God means and uses for our eternal good and the good of His people (see Genesis 50:15–21).

Back in Job, after chapters and chapters of Job's wrestling with the *whys* of his suffering, we get to chapter 38 when God, in His timing, answers Job, "Who is this that darkens counsel by words without knowledge?" (v. 2). God reminds Job for the next two chapters that He alone is God Almighty. He alone sees the beginning from the end and has power over every square inch of the earth. When Job comes face-to-face with the glorious rule of God, he replies, "Behold, I am of small account; what shall I answer You? I lay my hand on my mouth" (40:4). God continues to reveal His glorious reign and Job repents of his small vision and small faith. God then restores Job, blessing "the latter days of Job more than his beginning" (42:12).

Here's the truth we need to remember, especially when suffering knocks on life's door. The enemy can only go as far as the Father allows. And our Father God can be trusted. He has a plan. He's doing something *good* in the lives of His children for which we wouldn't even think to ask if left to us. And sometimes His *eternal good* plans include seasons of suffering. Seasons where we're stripped of everything this earth has to offer and we cling desperately to our God.

Paul knew the war would keep waging. He knew that until Jesus comes again, the enemies of God would continue their attacks on God's people *within the boundaries God sets*. He knew he needed the people of God to keep on praying for him to stand firm.

"Keep alert with all perseverance, making supplication for all the saints, and also for me, that words may be given to me in opening my mouth boldly to proclaim the mystery of the gospel" (Ephesians 6:18–19). Paul calls us to stay alert. The enemy prowls around. Stay on guard and pray continually. Pray that we would be bold in our declarations of the gospel.

Bold. Not mean. Not unloving. Not slaying the world with words of condemnation. But bold, which means "frankness; an unreservedness of utterance; confidence." Paul desires to engage the world with an inner confidence as he speaks of the love of Christ, even in the threat of death for such proclamations.

My local church always says to the volunteers, "May the gospel be the only offensive thing people encounter when they come to our gathering." We want the coffee hot. We want the parking lot friendly. We want the childcare safe. We want people of all walks of life to feel welcome. And then we pray that the gospel is spoken clearly and boldly so people have only one thing to grapple with: the gospel message. The gospel offends but God's people don't need to.

Just as Paul asked for prayer, we too need prayer. We need to pray for one another that we would stand firm in the midst of a spiritual war—a war in which the enemy wants us silenced. We need to pray that we would declare the gospel of Christ with confidence. We need to pray that we would be deeply rooted in the love that came down and changed us. And then that His love would confidently flow from our lips to others.

back to you

Why is it important to remember the limits of the enemy when suffering is great?

In what relationship or situation do you need to pray for boldness to speak the truth in love?

Based upon today's text, write a prayer for boldness in your own life.

What one thing from today's study do you want to remember?

DAY SIX
Ephesians 6:21–23

We made it! We made it to the last few verses of Paul's letter to the Ephesians. Getting to this last day is bittersweet for me personally. But as I write I pray God would grace you with a renewed passion as you finish up this letter from Paul. May we close these last pages with a fresh fire of faith to walk out our days pouring out the love of our Lord Jesus Christ on all who step on our path.

Read Ephesians 6:21–23. Write these verses in your journal.

What does today's text reveal about God?

God the Father:

God the Son (Jesus Christ):

God the Holy Spirit:

What does today's text reveal about humankind?

We're not meant to do life alone. We're not meant to live on the proverbial island. We're not meant to be the Lone Ranger. In fact, it can be dangerous to live life alone and guarded. God calls us to relationship. We're meant to be intertwined with other believers. We're meant to share our lives with our brothers and sisters. We need one another.

I can't tell you how many times the Lord has used physical people to spur me on in my faith. Our local church focuses upon its people being in a community group. A community group is just a group of people from our church that you commit to doing life beside. We share our struggles. We share our fears. We pray for each other. We laugh. We cry. We eat lots of cake and other sugary nuggets of goodness. And we spur each other on in this faith race—in this spiritual war.

We need one another.

That's why Paul wrote his letters. That's why he sent word to his many churches telling of his happenings. That's why he sent Tychicus to tell the Ephesians everything that was going on with him (Ephesians 6:21). We as God's people need each other. It encourages our hearts in this faith race when we hear of others running the race. It inspires us to get up and stand firm, sword raised high against the enemy, when we hear of others believing well.

Today we read the final greetings of Paul, and I'm reminded of how much I need my sisters and brothers in Christ. I need them to encourage my heart with word of their testimony in the midst of the war. Likewise, they too need my word of testimony as they fight their own battles.

You know what I notice in this text though? Paul doesn't tell *us* the details of his daily trials. We see the big picture. We read the truths that apply no matter the situation. But I would bet that Tychicus shared the more intimate happenings of Paul's everyday battles as he sat around the table with these Ephesian friends. And that's a word for us.

I may not share the exact details of my intimate battles with the world at large. I don't think I'm supposed to. But I know God gives us real life people with whom we're called to share our personal struggles. He places people in our lives with whom we're to have honest conversation over a meal or a cup of coffee. And then we encourage each other to keep on fighting the true enemy. We encourage one another as we testify to the faithfulness of God.

I have tears in my eyes as I sit here in this coffee shop typing out these final words. My soul prays deep things for you. I pray the love of our Lord and Savior Jesus Christ would go deep in you—that you would go deep in His love. I pray God would grace you with other believers with whom to run this race. I pray the enemy would think twice before launching those same old fiery darts at you because he knows he'll lose as you lift the shield and sword of God. I pray "peace be to [you, my sister], and love with faith, from God the Father and the Lord Jesus Christ. Grace be with you all who love our Lord Jesus Christ with love incorruptible" (Ephesians 6:23).

May you be deeply rooted in the immeasurable love of our good God.

back to you

Who has God given you to share in this walk of faith? Thank the Lord for each of them.

Why do we fear being vulnerable?

When has the faith of another encouraged your own heart to keep running your faith race?

What one thing from today's study do you want to remember?

NOTE TO SMALL GROUP LEADERS

Whether you've decided to walk through *Rooted* with a group of other women or you're just thinking about it, I'm so excited. I fully believe that we as daughters in Christ are designed to do life in community. We need each other. We need to be vulnerable with each other. We need to pray for one another and encourage one another.

In efforts to help you make your group discussion time most beneficial, I've listed some tips below. I pray your time with other women proves to be fruitful!

GATHER 8 TO 10 WOMEN INTO A GROUP.

- Have them each get a copy of the book before your first meet.
- Consider forming a private Facebook or other online social group to stay in communication with one another throughout the week. Here you could post the Scripture reading each day and ask for participants to "check in."
- Meet once per week in person to discuss the prior week's lesson.
- As the leader, be vulnerable. Share your own struggles, weaknesses, and journey. Vulnerability among your group will happen in direct proportion to your own vulnerability.

SUGGESTED SCHEDULE:

7:00–7:10 Gather, fellowship, and prayer.

7:10–7:55 Spend about 5–10 minutes reviewing each day. Asking people to share what blessed or affected them most for each day.

7:55–8:00 Have each participant write their prayer requests on a notecard and exchange them with a partner. Each partner should commit to pray for the other person over that next week.

8:00 Close with a general prayer and dismiss.

Some may want to linger and fellowship while others may need to leave due to other responsibilities. Encourage the ladies to stay connected through the week in person, by phone, or through your online social group.

I pray that God graciously uses the truths outlined in this book to root you and your ladies even deeper into His love.

~ *Lara*

If you enjoyed this book, will you consider sharing the message with others?

Let us know your thoughts at info@newhopepublishers.com. You can also let the author know by visiting or sharing a photo of the cover on our social media pages or leaving a review at a retailer's site. All of it helps us get the message out!

Twitter.com/NewHopeBooks

Facebook.com/NewHopePublishers

Instagram.com/NewHopePublishers

New Hope® Publishers is a division of Iron Stream Media, which derives its name from

> Proverbs 27:17, "As iron sharpens iron, so one person sharpens another."

This sharpening describes the process of discipleship, one to another. With this in mind, Iron Stream Media provides a variety of solutions for churches, missionaries, and nonprofits ranging from in-depth Bible study curriculum and Christian book publishing to custom publishing and consultative services. Through the popular Life Bible Study and Student Life Bible Study brands, ISM provides web-based full-year and short-term Bible study teaching plans as well as printed devotionals, Bibles, and discipleship curriculum.

For more information on ISM and New Hope Publishers, please visit

IronStreamMedia.com
NewHopePublishers.com